Living Together: More-than-Human Ecologies for Architectural Thinking

Sonal Mithal
Akshar Gajjar

Birkhäuser Basel

Foreword: In the Aftermath of the Devastation of Environment-Worlds

Hélène Frichot

I once fell in love with a rainbow lorikeet (*Psittacus moluccanus*), a bird native to Australia though considered a pest in such places as New Zealand. They are known for producing a cacophonous chorus as the sun rises and again as the sun sets as they prepare their perches for nighttime rest. My family and I called our psittacine visitor Lori, short for Lorikeet, the name my younger son gave our cross-species guest. Lori ended up with us as the result of a bird rescue mission. We discovered Lori, a quivering bundle of gray fuzz, some five weeks old, at the base of a Canary Island palm just outside our home. This was during the Covid-19 pandemic, when households were under conditions of lockdown and locals would spread out picnic blankets on the long grassy thoroughfare on our street as a means of seeking some reprieve. Early in 2020, this same street had borne witness to rolling waves of bushfire smoke creeping northward from the coast and reddening the sky. The brutal loss of cross-species life and the devastation of their environment-worlds was a horror to behold.

Resisting humanity's will to destruction, this ambitious co-authored volume argues that we are "living together" when seeking moments of leisure, love, and play with our cross-species companions. The question for our discipline is: What would architecture be like if we returned to a consideration of how to best share our environment-worlds?

Critics warn of the human aptitude for im posing anthropomorphic assumptions onto our cross-species companions. Assuming human characteristics in our pets, and the other nonhumans we are so fortunate to engage with, comes with the risk of misunderstanding what our companions are in fact thinking, feeling, and demanding in terms of quality of life. Concerning such matters, Jane Bennett, in her book *Vibrant Matter: A Political Ecology of Things* (2009), draws attention to an important distinction between anthropocentrism and anthropomorphism. Whereas the former centers the human subject as exceptional, at the apex of a pyramid of existence that has resulted in producing havoc and destruction for nonhumans, the latter can be situated as the speculative leap humans make to empathize, think, and coexist with cross-species companions.

Anthropomorphism, when resituated with care, can inaugurate expansive, collective imaginings, which enable humans to extend their sympathies beyond their kith and kin to the extraordinary diversity of beings with which we share this damaged planet. Cohabitative environments become a means of sharing and learning with one another across the taxonomic classifications that have divided species. We must, as a matter of urgency, extend our imaginations and transform our mere sympathies into deep ecological empathies. Engaging in shared matters of care, critical action might enable us to radically recalibrate our architectural and urban environments.

As the authors of this book argue, we need to find the means of centering architecture "as an agent for cohabitation and multispecies proliferation." Today, we discover ourselves in a situation of our own making amid a sixth mass-extinction event. We are the comet that has landed, we are the ice age that is arriving, we are the anthropogenic violence that has inflicted itself on this near-exhausted world. Extinction is not a singular event but reveals the entanglement and relations of dependency between humans and nonhumans. We must think not in the singular but with the mass noun: the flock, the committee, the parliament of things.

In the specific context of India, where this book situates itself, chains of ecological destruction can be witnessed unfurling. When the house sparrow and her family diminish in number, pest control goes awry, for these birds are no longer there to feed on insects and their larvae. When committees of vultures are decimated, falling victim to human pharmaceuticals that have gotten into the food chain, pathogens spread through urban environments, as animal carcasses are no longer cleaned from city streets. All such disappearances ecologically concatenate, wreaking death and destruction on webs of life.

Animal theorist Vinciane Despret contributes a haunting afterword to the anthology *Extinction Studies: Stories of Time, Death, and Generations* (2017) lamenting the end of the passenger pigeon (*Ectopistes migratorius*). When the passenger pigeon went extinct, not only did it disappear from the face of the earth, but a whole environment-world vanished. Despret imagines the genetic memory embodied in the bird and its kin, "the memory of massacres, rifles, and trees that people set in flames in the darkest of night." Their deep memory of a world now ruined, "the land, forests, and fields, seen by few eyes, no longer resembled anything [...] their patterns and colors, so familiar and recognizable when the eyes are many, had become incomprehensibly foreign and senseless for theirs" (Despret 2017, 218). The bird forms a collective subject: singular they make no sense, collaboratively they once inhabited a world now gone.

This book follows a feminist-materialist ecological inquiry, what I like to call dirty feminist materialism (Frichot 2023). It encourages us to pay attention to environment-worlds and acknowledge how plants and animals exercise their own agency. If only we architects would hesitate long enough to practice response-ability, to slow down, to step back, to give way to the sentience of nonhuman life. We must allow the world to become porous again and let the sky flood with wings.

Lori the lorikeet showed me and my family some of these things during the fourteen or so weeks our feathered friend rested with us. Lori showed us the importance of care, the challenges of cohabiting, the grief that comes when we must let go and give up our aspiration for control. One day, sunning ourselves on the upstairs terrace, Lori took flight and never returned. The rainbow lorikeet is not in threat of extinction, but when Lori left us what remained was a profound sense of grief, as if a whole world were slipping out of view.

Introduction

Figure 0.1 Pigeon dwellings incorporated into human habitats in the Mughal towns of India. Illustration from Valih Musavi's *Kabutarnama,* 1788.

Figure 0.2 Pigeons are part of a courtly woman's leisure event. Opaque watercolor on paper, unknown artist, c. 1760s.

Kabutarnama, a book on the art of pigeon-keeping written and illustrated by Valih Musavi in 1788, includes several depictions of contemporaneous pigeon dwellings that were incorporated into human habitats in the Mughal towns of North India. Cotes, niches, cages, ledges, feeders, and small water tanks are seen integrated into terraces, external walls, parapets, and archways. These images speak of the existing and effortless culture of accommodating multispecies habitats within the creation of architecture. In one of the paintings by Musavi, *A Courtyard Filled with Pigeons* (1788), pigeons occupy more canvas area than humans **Fig 0.1**. In another, *A Lady Smoking a Huqqa and Watching Pigeons* (unknown artist, c. 1760s), pigeons occupy the center of the frame **Fig 0.2**. In the background is an elaborate rectilinear three-storied dovecote, a portable structure with tiny arched openings for pigeons to perch in. The painting suggests that the birds and the humans are sharing a restful evening on the terrace of a royal house. Sharing moments of leisure indicates a departure from utilitarian purposes toward the social, or inter-species epitome of cohabitation. The presence and representation of pigeons within human-made architecture historically and culturally prompts us to trace the actions that led to a loss of such environments of cohabitation. With an awareness that pigeons are a highly adaptable species and extremely invasive, *Living Together* foregrounds these examples to extend the cohabitative environments of humans and more-than-humans to include other urban species and speculate what that architecture would be like.

Modern architecture has prioritized human exclusivity to such an extent that ecological interrelationships have become obscured. The construction of an architectural project is initiated with the clearing and cleansing of the construction site, interfering with the existing more-than-human relationships on the site and disrupting them at local and ecosystemic scales. Foundations are dug in this tabula rasa, overturning organic matter that hosts myriad visible and invisible species. Other life-forms and habitats are obliterated. We argue that the development of such modern architecture has been instrumental in creating the threat of mass extinction in cities that we face today. Modernity has taught us that exclusively living apart from other species and exploiting natural resources has only been detrimental to human habitation. Hence, a renewed urgency is emerging that calls on us to reconsider this distancing and imagine human and nonhuman worlds as coinciding. Positioning itself in this conversation, *Living Together* centers architecture as an agent for cohabitation and multispecies proliferation.

Species extinction rates have sharply increased in the last two hundred years, corresponding to the rise of industrial society and urbanization (Ceballos et al. 2015, 3). In the last decade, there has been a significant rise in the global population of urban dwellers.[1] The resultant urban development has had an antithetical relationship with the more-than-human population. Placing images such as those by Musavi in the context of the ongoing species crisis lends visibility to how architecture has been instrumental in becoming a threshold of cohabitation between the human and the more-than-human. The modernization of architecture reduced its capacity to interweave humans and more-than-humans, with the former affecting the survival of the latter. When a species is lost, larger biological systems, food systems, ecological systems, social systems, and cultural systems tied to the overall ecology are affected. Species loss is complex and something we can't afford, as it affects the overall ecology on which even human survival depends. In India, as many as 99 species of mammals, 88 bird species, 106 reptile species, 139 amphibian species, 328 fish species, and 603 plant species are endangered owing to urbanization.[2] One of the largest victims of Indian urbanization has been the house sparrow (*Passer domesticus*) (Sharma and Binner 2020, 1). This decline is due to the loss of nesting opportunities and soil surfaces, essential parts of the bird's life cycle, in the overly paved cityscapes. The lives of humans and house sparrows are intrinsically linked: sparrows maintain the ecosystem balance by feeding on insects and larvae, thus acting as natural pest control, and by pollinating plants. Furthermore, solitary bees (*Halictus scabiosae, Xylocopa violacea*) face the threat of urban extinction owing to the replacement of porous construction materials such as bamboo, wood, and mud with hard surfaces like concrete, plaster, brick, and stone, reducing nesting opportunities. They play a significant role in maintaining food security for humans and are far more effective as pollinators compared to honeybees (Khalifa et al. 2021, 7). Vultures are essential because of their efficiency in eating dead animals quickly and cleanly, containing the spread of diseases and lowering human mortality.[3] Their population has declined by almost 95 percent—they have been dying off because the anti-inflammatory drug Diclofenac is present in the carcasses (Frank and Sudarshan 2023, 4).[4] This decline has resulted in the spread of pathogens and the contamination of bodies of water, as feral dogs and rats—the primary carriers of rabies—leave behind flesh when they consume carcasses, which is unsanitary (Frank

1 An increase from 52.5 percent in 2012 to 56.9 percent in 2022, with 68 percent by 2050 predicted (UN DESA 2018).

2 The International Union for Conservation of Nature's red list of endangered plant and animal species includes the hog deer (*Axis porcinus*), king cobra (*Ophiophagus hannah*), wild water buffalo (Bubalus arnee), barasingha (*Rucervus duvaucelii*), hispid hare (*Caprolagus hispidus*), woolly flying squirrel (*Eupetaurus cinereus*), capped langur (*Trachypithecus pileatus*), cinnamon (*Cinnamomum sulphuratum*), hill turmeric (*Curcuma pseudomontana*), mitha guggul (*Commiphora stocksiana*), yellow-throated bulbul (*Pycnonotus xantholaemus*), white-bellied heron (*Ardea insignis*), forest owlet (*Athene blewitti*), Indian vulture (*Gyps indicus*), eastern imperial eagle (*Aquila heliaca*), yellow-eyed pigeon (*Columba eversmanni*), and house sparrow (*Passer domesticus*) (IUCN 2024).

3 Vultures can reduce a cow carcass to bone in about forty minutes (Frank and Sudarshan 2023, 7).

4 In 1994 Diclofenac, a common painkiller, began being prescribed to treat livestock. The medicine would remain in the body of the animal and hence the carcass.

5 A recent study has estimated that within the last 120 years, the mass of human-made material—of which concrete and aggregate amount to 50 percent—has surpassed the total biomass of earth (Elhacham et al. 2020, 443).

and Sudarshan 2023, 7). These are among the many instances that illustrate how human lives are interwoven with the lives of the more-than-human; how extinction is not a singular nor an isolated event; and how the extinction of one species impacts, and at times threatens, the sustenance of another.

With their roots in modernism, architecture and the construction industry are at the center of this ongoing urban mass extinction. A substantial increase in construction material mass has directly impacted the lives of diverse species through writing over and erasing their habitats, which is one of the main drivers of spiking extinction rates.[5] Modern architecture was born out of modern architects' fear of illness, predominantly tuberculosis, and the architecture they devised represented a cure (Colomina 2019, 18, 93). These architects followed their doctors' prescriptions for habitats free of dust, pollen, and insects, which became part of their working drawings for various projects such as residences, asylums, hospitals, and health clubs. Architects and thinkers such as Paul Scheerbart began to consider building materials from the dimension of health and sought doctors who would endorse his polemic against the use of brick, which he considered unhygienic (Colomina 2019, 86). In one of Scheerbart's architectural imaginings, he advocates for glass, light, and color, and imagines an airship high above from where humans could observe animals (Scheerbart 2001, 44–49) Fig 0.3. Modernity distanced humans and other species in the name of sanitation and hygiene. This obsession with sanitary environments was also extended to the immediate surroundings of human dwellings, eliminating urban wildlife.

Given the urgency of cohabitation as a strategy, emerging architectural imaginations—some experimental, some speculative, some artistic—are either quite literal in mimicking other-than-human habitats or have humanized the habitats for other species. Some architects have recently taken this call for extending voice to more-than-humans seriously and are building systems to be integrated into architectural practice and thinking. Recognizing architecture's reliance on anthropometric standards and anthropomorphic norms of spatial layouts, the Berlin-based architectural studio Animal-Aided Design has been inventorying detailed life-cycle portraits of various bird and animal species present in or endangered by urban environments. Just as architects consult anthropometric standards, this inventory can be used to integrate specific conditions to support multispecies habitats. If consulted with care and restraint, such inventories can be useful for designing conditions where more-than-humans can nest on their own without prescribing solutions. Conceived by the EU project Horizon 2020 FET Open (Future and Emerging Technologies), ECOLOPES

Figure 0.3 A distancing of humans and animals in Paul Scheerbart's modern architecture.

(ECOlogical building enveLOPES) go a step further, advocating for the need to conceive architectural designs that integrate multispecies habitat requirements from the very beginning. Not distinguishing the human from the more-than-human, ECOLOPES are tailor-made multispecies habitats for various plants, animals, microbiota, and humans. Dynamics of interspecies interactions and their relationships to the environment are fed as data to architectural design systems to generate iterative designs (Perini et al. 2021, 371; Selvan et al. 2023).

It doesn't require big gestures to create cohabitative architecture; simple, matter-of-fact, everyday gestures that can be made by one and all are sufficient. Housing solitary bees is one such opportunity. With urbanization, natural permeable surfaces are replaced by impermeable materials, reducing nesting sites for solitary bees.[6] To host solitary bees, all that is required are hollow wooden or bamboo sticks tied together and hung for the cavity-nesting bees, and some soil left free in unpaved gardens for the ground-nesting species (Kumar-Rao 2021). This act to build biodiversity can be achieved by any ordinary city resident. To proliferate bees in an effortless way, ATREE (Ashoka Trust for Research in Ecology and the Environment, Bangalore) designed a two-foot-high porous wooden structure called the Bee Hotel, which can be easily installed in private gardens and on balconies and terraces.[7] Similarly, Space10 created the open-source Bee Home.[8] These digitally fabricated blocks with holes can be assembled by users, encouraging the integration of bee habitats into urban areas. Likewise, Faye Clifton has designed the Bee Brick—a block with cavities that replaces a brick in the wall, providing a nesting place for several species of solitary bees.[9]

These projects have stemmed from a growing awareness that human dominance and exploitation of other species have been detrimental to humanity's own well-being and survival. Their various approaches take new theoretical standpoints, integrate technocentric strategies, and implement civic-action programs. The projects have focused on a deep reading of bird habitats, bee habitats, and biological invasion in abandoned areas. The intention is to increase our knowledge of how more-than-human species live and thrive, which can be integrated into our built environment. Consequently, there is an emerging awareness that coexistence with other species is crucial at this point.

6 Studies done at the Entomology Department at Gandhi Krishi Vigyan Kendra and the Indian Institute of Science Education and Research Trivandrum have revealed that solitary bees thrive in urban gardens, hence food is not an issue (Kumar-Rao 2021). These bees tend to live separately, as their name suggests. The female bees build burrows or bore holes close to one another. Carpenter bees carve holes into wood or bamboo with their powerful mandibles. Mason bees, blue-banded bees, and leaf-cutter bees burrow into mud or nest in small cavities.

7 The Bee Hotel accommodates varying kinds of bee species found in Bangalore and southeastern Karnataka. The top section has premade holes for bees to nest safely; the middle section acts like a structural support system with bamboo sticks; the bottom section is an empty space to fill with soil. In April 2022, 50 Bee Hotels were installed in Bangalore (Mathew 2022).

8 Space10, a Copenhagen-based design firm, designed the Bee Home in collaboration with Tanita Klein and Bakken & Bæck.

9 Clifton runs the UK-based company Green&Blue, which manufactures Bee Bricks (Souza 2022).

Increasingly, the artists and architects are drawing on feminist ecological scholarship, specifically by Donna Haraway. For example, Superflux's installation *Refuge for Resurgence* (2021) drew on Haraway's "string figure" imagery (Haraway 2016b, 9) to conceptualize a dining table where various species sit together for a meal.[10] The artists' choice of a dining table reveals their intention of challenging the hierarchies of a food chain. Eating together at the table subverts hierarchies and requires diners to share resources and negotiate. However, the dining table is anthropometric, visible in the snakeskin-covered tree-stump seats, something a human would use, or a raven sculpture placed on a bough away from the table. In the use of anthropometric furniture and the form of formal dining, we read a tension between the human agency that choreographs such scenarios and the agreement of the other-than-human species to participate in it. A similar tension between humans visu-

10 Responding to the theme "How We Live Together" at the 17th Architectural Exhibition in Venice in 2021, the dining table is conceptualized as a multispecies banquet taking place after the end of the world. The table is laid with various dining tools that can be used by a fox, rat, wasp, pigeon, cow, human adult and child, wild boar, snake, beaver, wolf, raven, and mushroom to dine together "around a majestic oak table". (Jain and Arden 2021).

Figure 0.4 ***Parliament of Plants.***

11 Situated in Socrates Park, New York, the project offers a habitat for endangered local species such as the Carolina wren and solitary bees (Harrison 2017).

alizing future cohabitative environments and the lack of agency afforded to more-than-human species is evident in Ariane Lourie Harrison's *The Birds and the Bees* (2016). The pavilion provides a system that automatizes the removal of bird feces from nests, mirroring the flushing systems of toilets.[11] The project aims to protect birds who are exposed to scavengers when they clean their nests. Even though well intentioned, it relies on anthropometric notions of comfort and safety. It ignores the fact that part of the bird's life is to clean their nest; if that activity is taken away, an imbalance sets in. This prompts the question of how and why the birds should adapt to this new environment of self-flushing systems.

Bruno Latour's "Parliament of Things" calls for creating platforms where those muted during the modernity project—nature and nonhuman objects—can voice their concerns (Latour 1993, 143). Critiquing the modernist paradigm, Latour highlights the supremacy of the human scientists who have been representing the nonhuman constituents of the earth for a human audience. It is a response to the divide between nature and culture propelled under the modernism paradigm. Similarly, Céline Baumann's *Parliament of Plants* (2019) acknowledges the intelligence of flora in proliferating an environment of mutual care and support (Baumann and Pohl 2020, 79) **Fig 0.4**. Drawing on Haraway and Tsing, Baumann subverts human-created power dynamics and relocates the responsibility of environmental care, putting plants in charge.

What does it mean for architecture when plants and other species exercise their own agency? Architecture would become truly receptive—both physically, premised on creating spaces for accommodating other-than-humans, and intellectually, premised on becoming aware of the needs of species other-than-human. Architecture would have to draw the line between providing for other-than-human species and allowing them to exercise their agency to construct their own habitat. It is time to stop architecting and let other species do their bit and make architecture a truly collaborative venture. However, when approached from a solutionist perspective for a particular species, such initiatives risk being patchy and hyper-specific, whereas when integrated with contemporary technologies, they risk being technocratic. The concern for cohabitative environments cannot be addressed by architectural design alone. However, a largely theoretical approach might be difficult to translate into design parameters. Design-based approaches, whether technocratic or demonstrating a theoretical standpoint, demand a holistic rather than a fragmented approach.

Living Together positions itself in that fragmentation, interweaving threads from feminist thinking and architectural initiatives. It advocates for more comprehensive ways of mapping multispecies habitats and demonstrates how that knowledge can be used in design, turning to two influential texts of the past decade: Donna Haraway's *Staying with the Trouble* (2016) and Anna Tsing's *The Mushroom at the End of the World* (2015). Haraway envisages a *terrapolis,* where various environmental actors constantly negotiate with one another to create cohabitational worlds, which could bolster architecture's capacity to initiate collaborative models of design and construction. Tsing considers human disturbance necessary for ecological continuities, which reminds us that humans participate in the multispecies project as much as nonhuman actors, foregrounding the necessity to make architecture proactive and holistic.

Undertaking a close reading of additional seminal works such as Gilles Deleuze and Félix Guattari's *A Thousand Plateaus* (1980), Manuel DeLanda's *A New Philosophy of Society* (2006), and Mary Douglas's *Purity and Danger* (1966), this book takes a nuanced look at the meanings of assemblage, terrapolis, and ruins from a materialist perspective. Through this exercise, we propose that architectural sites and objects operate within existing codependencies and hence need to be liberated from determinism. We develop a vocabulary based on materialism for architects to make ecological codependencies integral to architecture. Studying the material characteristics of ruins, this book argues that they are characterized by tentacularity, hybridity, vacancy, receptivity, indeterminacy, and networks—characteristics that have an innate capacity to become architectural as well. A perspectival shift in understanding the relation between humans and more-than-humans is required, based on the consideration that nonhumans have agency and all entities are products of their material qualities, which define the dynamics of interspecies relationships—the materiality of spatial factors in which such dynamics take place.

Living Together is an inquiry into an architecture that allows multispecies alliances to take place. It brings feminist-materialist ecological inquiries to architectural design, practice, and thinking, acknowledging the necessity of subverting established architectural practices of progress, monumentality, longevity, and permanence. In that subversion, manifold possibilities emerge for self-organized, ecologically resilient built environments; feminist ecology mobilizes a multispecies collaborative survival for architecture. *Living Together* takes the post-industrial ruin as its object of study. When abandoned by humans, the more-than-human species already present in the structures start to become visible.

The idea of the book began with a series of architectural design studios led by Sonal Mithal at CEPT University in Ahmedabad between 2018 and 2023: "Terrain-Vague Bricolage" (2018, 2019), "Ecotone: The Sentient Ruins" (2021), and "Staging Ecologies" (2022, 2023). "Ecotone: The Sentient Ruins" invited participants to propose an *ecotone architecture*—architecture that acts as an inorganic component of a post-industrial landscape and facilitates a multispecies habitat. Ecotone comprises the zone where two landscape patterns or habitats overlap, forming a transition between two sets of biophysical and cultural elements, relationships, and processes. Understanding the nature of nonhuman workings, the series of studios proposed architectural interventions for the ecological recovery of abandoned sites in India: the Pickers Mill and the New Commercial Mill in Ahmedabad (2018), basalt quarries in Champaner (2019, 2021), and abandoned urban precincts in Qaiserbagh (2022, 2023). While contributing to the local economy, these architectural proposals acknowledged the agency of ecological forces on the site that would continuously subvert the projects. Architecture was imagined as an agent that would contribute to the new ecosystem by being adaptable—maintaining, increasing, and assisting its constant mutation. Ecologically responsive material-specific forms were proposed, some of which are featured in this book.

The aim of the studios was to identify the adaptive potential of architecture in the midst of climate change. To do that, the studios focused on evaluating and presenting post-industrial landscapes as *sentient ruins*—a system of elements, human conditions, and material resources that offer a precedent for adaptable systems that can be appropriated into architectural thinking. The studios established a relationship among the seemingly fragmented conditions of the sentient ruin, such as the decay in organic matter, fractures in the stone caused by quarrying, evidence of the coexistence of igneous and sedimentary rocks, and the presence of emerging vegetation in the cracks of the cliff. Drawing on feminist-materialist thinking, the studios explored the question of survival by discovering what manages to live (and how) in the ruins of such a landscape, looking for evidence of multispecies collaborative survival. They proposed reappropriating and remodeling the distressed components of an abandoned quarry to be a place for ecological recovery. The studios underscored the fact that ruins reflect the exploitation of natural resources until their limits are reached, arguing that the processes that have endured because of multispecies interdependence offer precedents for architectural thinking and practice. To undertake a deep reading of the sites' multispecies workings, the studios developed parameters and methods they termed *mapping sentience*. This approach has contributed significantly to this book's chapter "Mapping the Sentient Ruin."

26

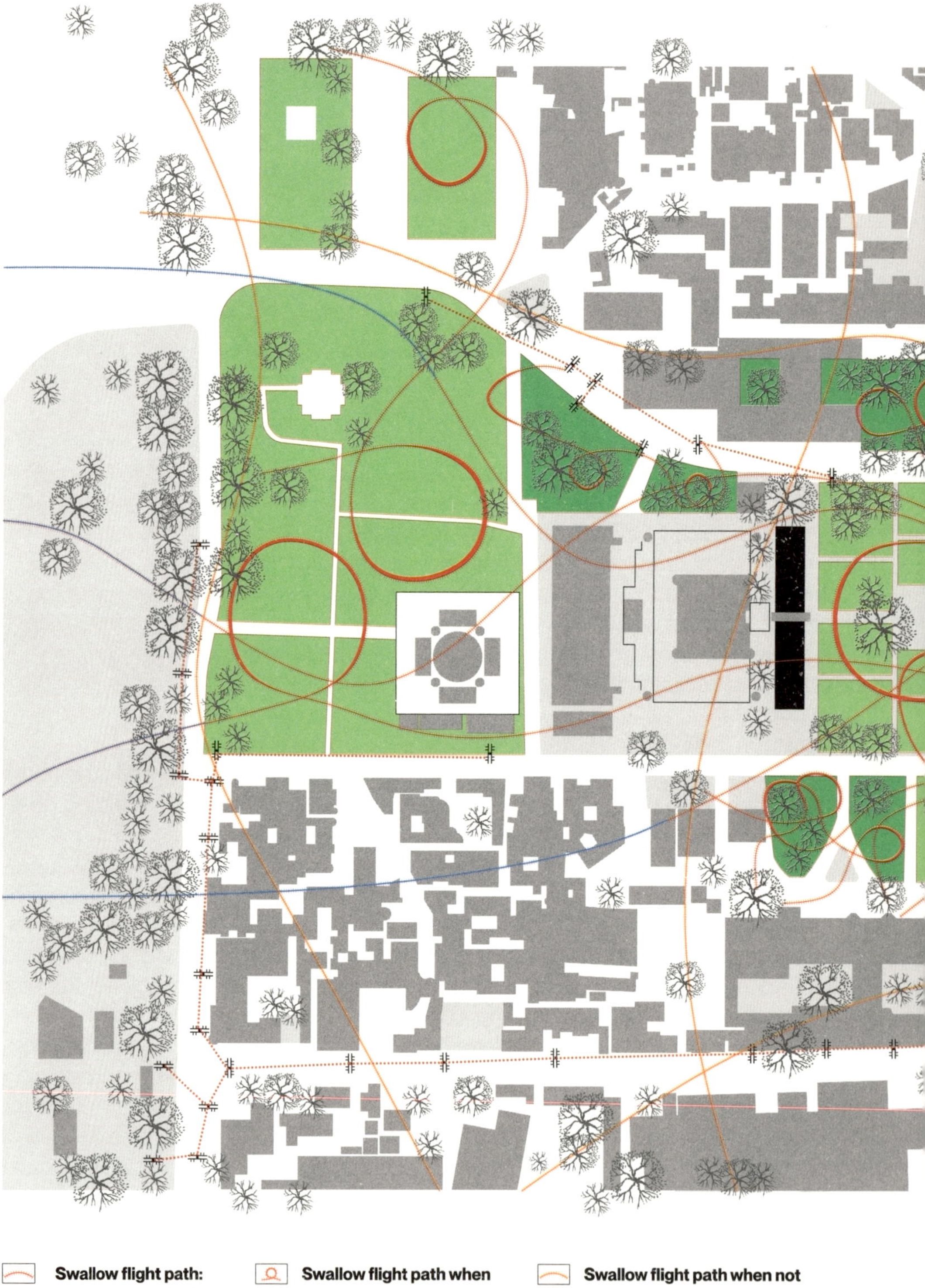

Swallow flight path: 4.2m–0.3m altitude

Swallow flight path when foraging at open grounds: 4.2m–0.3m altitude

Swallow flight path when not foraging: altitude > 4.2m

Figure 0.5 a Barn swallow flight paths at Qaiserbagh in Lucknow, India.

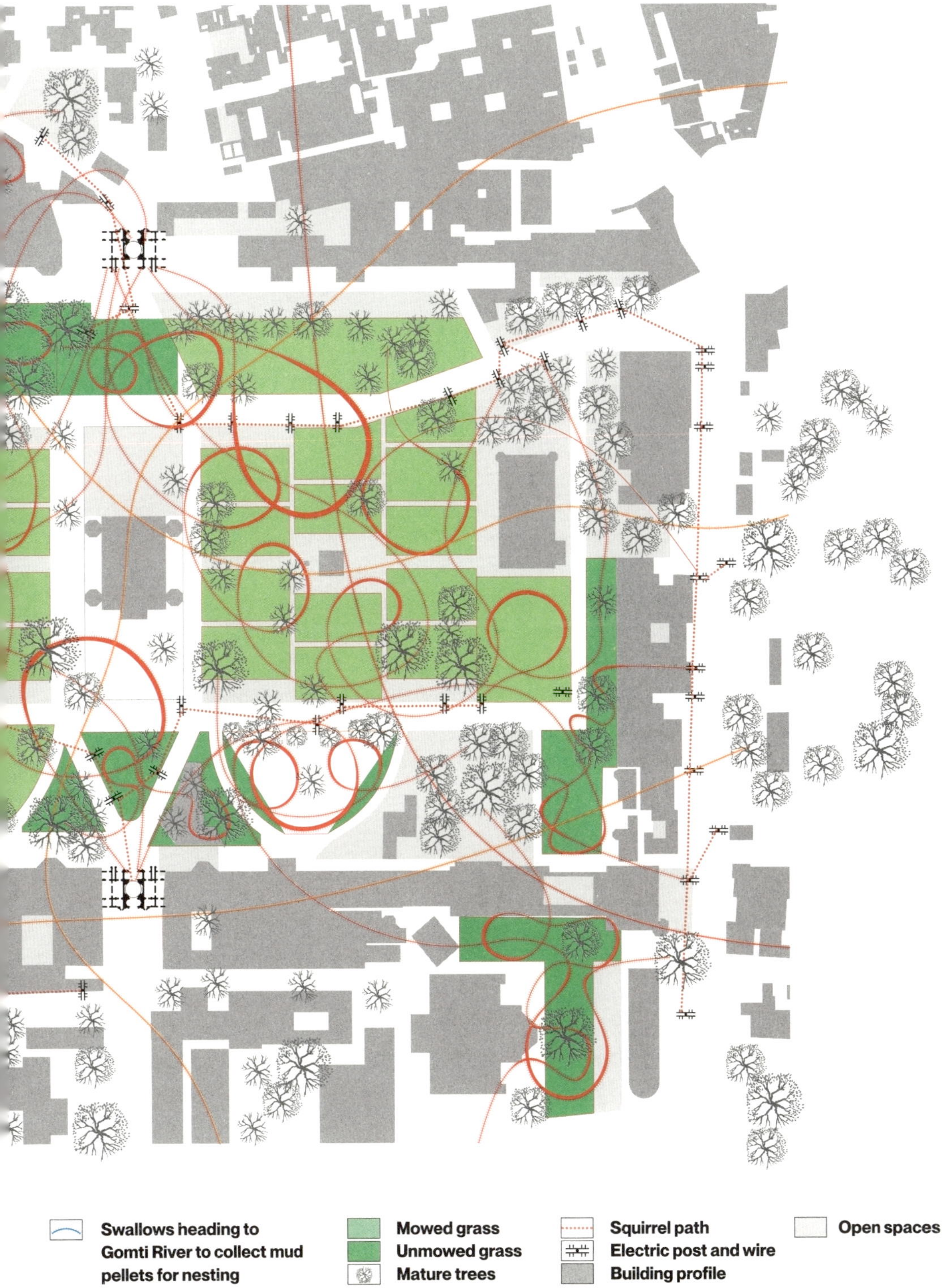

Akshar Gajjar's bachelor thesis in architecture at CEPT University is a critique of anthropocentrism in architectural thinking, especially the way it reads and maps the environment (2021). This work had two aims: to derive parameters for a multispecies reading of the built environment and to inquire how such a reading can inform architectural-design thinking. Stemming from Haraway's entanglements of tentacular beings (Haraway 2016b, 31) and Tsing's art of paying attention (Tsing 2015, 24), the thesis developed a new perspective for looking at interspecies relationships to move away from a solutionist approach and derived spatial parameters for mapping multispecies relationships on-site. To demonstrate this method, the thesis conducted a four-fold mapping of the ruins of the New Commercial Mill in Ahmedabad. Mapping the mill's walls and roof inferred that plant growth on ruin surfaces often make architecture resilient. Mapping the surface, animals, and birds illustrated how urban wildlife exercises agency in creating a habitat in the walls and on the roof. Mapping networks revealed that architecture does not stand in isolation but collaborates with proximate plant species to form systems of multispecies movements and habitats. Lastly, mapping dirt showed that waste matter supports habitat making, food foraging, and the daily activities of various birds, insects, and rodents. The semester-long thesis project concluded by highlighting the urgency to include more-than-humans in the urban built environment and attempted to propose parameters of mapping that can support such an inclusion. *Living Together* brings together the work done in Mithal's studios and Gajjar's thesis and extends the arguments to think of cohabitative architectural acts for the future.

In a study undertaken for the studio "Staging Ecologies," Jaikishore A. mapped the unique flight path of barn swallows in relation to the gardens of the historic Qaiserbagh palace complex in Lucknow. From on-site observations and other references, he inferred that these birds feed exclusively in flight, foraging for insects by flying in loops close to the ground. This activity intensifies over unmown grass, which attracts larger swarms of insects. The flight paths suggest prey capture if they have sharp bends or loops; a relatively straight flight path means the bird is flying at a higher altitude, possibly migrating. One drawing shows an overlaying of flight patterns with the mowed and unmowed open grounds of Qaiserbagh **Fig 0.5 a**. Naturally skilled masons, barn swallows use a mix of clay, dried grass, and feathers to make pellets that are layered to form their cup nests. The most preferred spots for their nests, as suggested by the maps, are enclosed spaces in dimly lit wooden ceilings that are not within human reach, especially in one of the historic structures of the Qaiserbagh known as Lakhi Gate. To make their nests, swallows collect clay from the Gomti River approximately a mile away. The urban nature of Qaiserbagh, with a combination of large swathes of manicured and naturally kept gardens, is conducive to a large population of barn swallows. The nesting behavior of barn swallows in the ruins of Lakhi Gate **Fig 0.5 b** shows the favorable

Figure 0.5 b Barn swallow nesting patterns at Qaiserbagh in Lucknow, India.

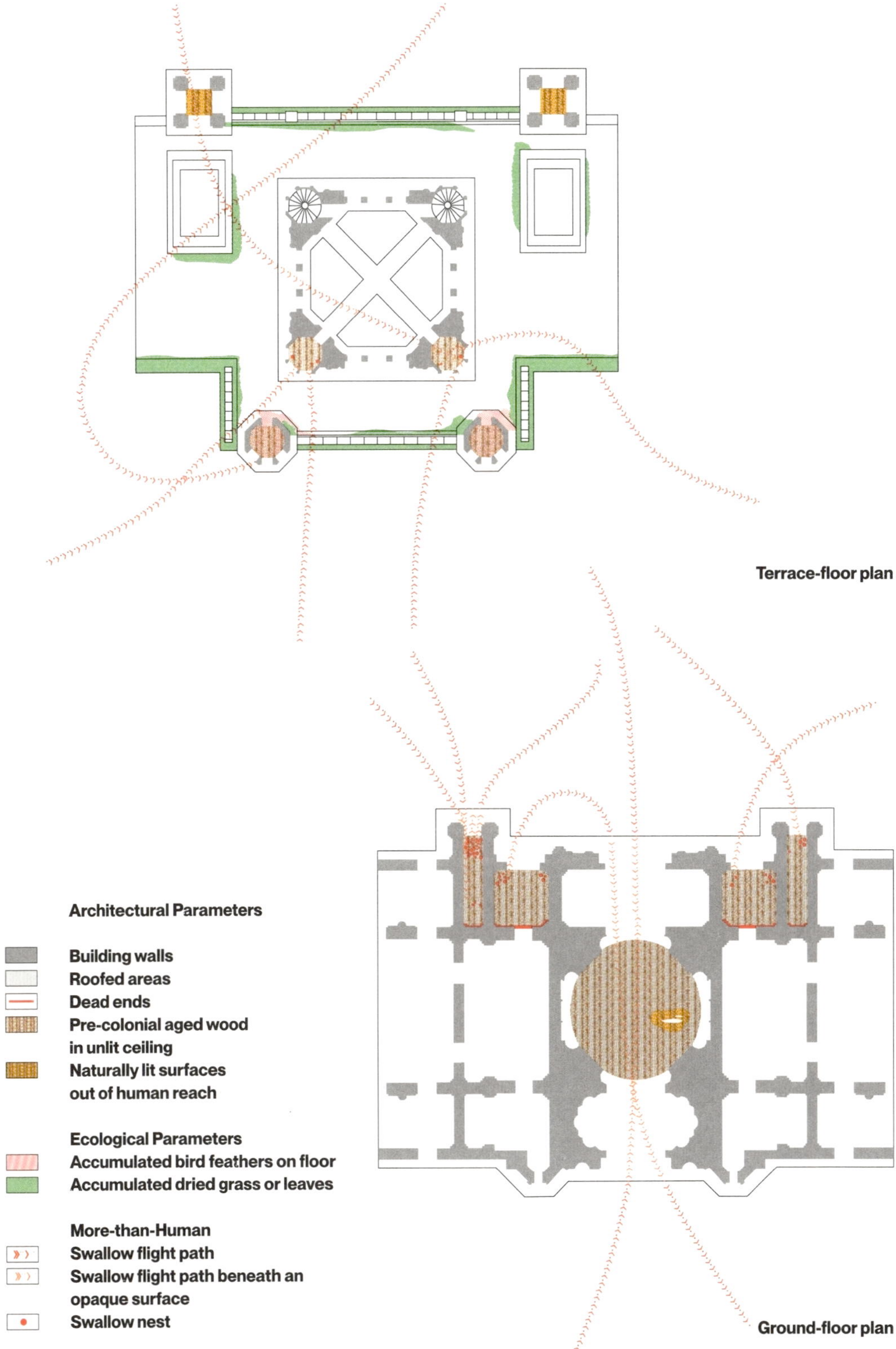

conditions for the nests, namely the ceiling material in which nests are built, the height of the ceiling, the amount of natural light, and the placement and patterns of various nesting materials. The study revealed that swallows nested in the rotting wood in the high ceiling of the brick gate, where it is damp, dark, and where no human or squirrel would venture, showing animals' intelligence in finding their own spaces and the conditions conducive to nesting and thriving. This research infers that architectural design does not need to focus on "providing" for other-than-humans but should let them live alongside humans without either intruding on the other.

Architectural elements such as walls have spatialized, and literally concretized, the divide between humans and their surroundings, increasing the distance between humans and the ecological components on which they depend. Haraway's concept of nature-cultures has called for the disruption of this separation (Haraway 2016a, 108). If a modernist wall made of concrete or glass has strengthened the divide, reimagining the wall differently can blur it. Haraway sees the figure of the cyborg as sitting on the fence, transcending boundaries, inhabiting and merging various worlds (Haraway 2016a, 7). A wall is an architectural component that, if reimagined, has the potential to become an interface for cyborgian habitation—the wattle and daub rammed-earth system, for example, which holds insects and microorganisms.

Not just the walls, but any external surface of a human habitat has the potential to become an ecotone—a transition zone between two or more biological communities. For example, permeability in floors has been a part of traditional housing in difficult landscapes, enhancing human and animal cohabitation. The Deoris, who reside on the Majuli riverine delta in Assam, adapt their houses to the wetland ecology of the region. Responding to the frequency of flash floods, houses are built using materials such as wood, bamboo, cane, reed, and thatch, in the form of raised-platform hutments known as Chang Ghar (Salam and Dasgupta 2021, 2093). The lower part of the house is used as an enclosure for animals. The higher temperatures of the lower section provide animals with the necessary warmth; the floor of the upper story is perforated for ventilation and to serve as an interface to pass food to the animals (Salam and Dasgupta 2021, 2094) **Fig 0.6**. Chang Ghar echoes Haraway's cyborg and helps to reimagine the ecotone literally, architecturally, and metaphorically.

Chapter 1, "Life in Ruins: A Multispecies Alliance," centers the discussion on ruins or sites of distress—sites left unattended for various reasons, from post-industrialization to conflicts over property ownership. These create opportunities for nonhumans to assume agency and manifest their survival in ways that exceed human control and benefit from passive human presence. The chapter discusses the nature, characteristics, and eventualities of multispecies collaborative survival within ruins, sites that subvert colonial and modernist progress-oriented construction practices. Chapter 2, "From Feminist Ecologies to Architectural Thinking: Formulating a Vocabulary," assembles critical texts related to feminist ecology, materialism, and phenomenology to create a terminology that transforms traditional architectural discourse, prioritizing the dirty over the sterile, the hybrid over the typological. The chapter proposes ways in which this approach is instrumental for deriving architectural forms and acts that support multispecies cohabitation. It undertakes a translation and unpacking of feminist-materialist terminologies into tangible parameters such as hybridity, the renewal/ruination dichotomy, fragility, and vacancy, which permit the reading and mapping

Figure 0.6 Perforated wood flooring in the Chang Ghar of the Deori community on Majuli Island, India.

of multispecies collaborations. These parameters become architectural tools to trace conditions that allow ruins to support such collaborative survival. In Chapter 3, "Mapping the Sentient Ruin," the book extends the parameters derived in the previous chapter to systematically map the presence and capacities of more-than-human species in adapting to human environments. It initiates a feminist reading, following Haraway's *Staying with the Trouble* especially, to discover what makes the ruins response-able to the species that are present, what makes the ruins a terrapolis, and how various human–nonhuman agencies are in a persistent state of queering the ruins. Mapping, here, is an outcome of the embodied experience of being in and of the site, combined with attention to various life-forms on the site. Three post-industrial abandoned sites are mapped: two abandoned textile mills in Ahmedabad and an abandoned basalt quarry in Champaner. Chapter 4, "Ecotone Architecture: Articulations of Posthumanist Elemental Assemblages," outlines six architectural lessons learned from mapping sentience in ruins for both site reading and architectural interventions. In their reading, they use tentacular thinking and prioritize irregularity, indeterminacy, hybridity, and networks in architecture. Furthermore, the chapter provides a survey of contemporary architectural projects and techniques—both built and conceptual—that foster, or have the potential to foster, multispecies architecture. Some projects featured in this chapter were developed as part of the series of studios led by Mithal between 2018 and 2023 at CEPT University.

Living Together details an imagination of architecture that can situate itself in intrinsic multispecies networks and actively participate as a human component.

1 Life in Ruins: A Multispecies Alliance

A disused brick structure in the military cantonment of Dehradun betrays a newfound structural language owing to its abandoned state. Originally built in the mid 1920s to supply water to the neighborhood, the upper floor housed a rectilinear brick trough as a water tank, and the brick arches of the ground floor supported the weight of both the building and water. However, after water pumps were installed in individual houses, the water tank became redundant. The water remaining in the brick trough and the deterioration of the damp-proof course started to encourage vegetal growth. Today, a composite of tree roots holds the brick structure, weaving a beautiful trellis-like pattern Fig 1.1. The invading tree appears to be strengthening rather than weakening the structure. The fusion prompts us to think about the potential of a ruin to redefine the rules of architecture's structural stability. Vegetation is usually removed as a first gesture in architectural conservation practices, but in the absence of human management, a hybrid of tree and brick emerges that ensures its own longevity. It is a ruin. Never empty, ruins are inhabited by multiple life-forms. No longer working as it was intended, a ruin "liberates function from its subservience to purpose," where "anarchy marches in" (Ginsberg 2004, 33).

Ruins become places where wilderness flourishes. The rules of the human world do not apply to ruins; ruins rather alienate humans, unless the humans agree with the terms of the new rules. Ruins are never static but always in a process of ruination. Thus, ruins are always open to their own perpetration, available to change, reinventing themselves. A ruin refers to the physical disintegration of a physical object, often an architectural one. To be in a state of ruin is to be in a state of disrepair, to be derelict, falling apart, dilapidated, decaying, neglected, uncared for, destroyed, broken. It is often a result of abandonment due to a natural calamity, political conflict, economic decline, conflicts over ownership, or movements of populations. In the human perspective of progress, a ruin has a negative connotation, as it emerges when humans stop caring for it. Ruins stand for the antithesis to growth, development, construction, and modernity.[1] During the Renaissance, a ruin aesthetic emerged, visualized in paintings and versed in poems about abandoned monuments taken over by vegetation, which allowed the European elite to indulge in a melancholic view of a lost past. It lamented the loss of something valuable representing human achievements, now a victim of destruction. However, precisely because of the absence of humans, the ruins take on a new meaning. Ruins have the capacity to subvert the colonial and progress-oriented modernist worldview.

1 The word ruin comes from the Latin *ruere* (to fall) and *ruina* (collapse), and from the Greek words *olethros* and *ereipion*, which mean torn down, fallen, wreck, destruction, or death (Ginsberg 2004, 286). Common antonyms for ruins include accomplishment, birth, building, construction, creation, and success.

Passing through an urban landscape, one might come across abandoned railroad tracks and neglected backyards or plots of land that have been claimed by wild plant growth. Such places are tucked into the built fabric or occupy its margins. An unexpected amount of biodiversity is observed in such spaces of abandonment. Calling attention to the ecological capacity of these spaces, the landscape architect Gilles Clément terms them the third landscape—unexploitable by machines, they host some of the

Figure 1.1 Tree having taken over an abandoned brick water tank in Dehradun, India.

most vulnerable and biodiverse species of their region (Clément 2015, 84). Acknowledging the "exploitative pasts" of such sites, Clément reads them as post-industrial ruins (Clément 2015, 148). In his 2009 project *Le Jardin du Tiers-Paysage* (*The Garden of the Third Landscape*), located on and within the roof of an abandoned submarine base in Saint-Nazaire, France, Clément invites nature to take over and complete a design he initiated. The project demonstrates the agency accorded to more-than-human species in leftover spaces. It is a project of three gardens—the Garden of Aspen Woods, the Garden of Stonecrops and Grasses, and the Garden of Labels—which proliferate on the dry concrete roof without major artificial maintenance. The roof of the submarine base has impressive dimensions of 126 × 300 meters. Built by the Germans between 1941 and 1942 to protect their submarines from attack, the seventeen-meter-deep roof has three layers—a two-meter-thick concrete base, a two-meter-deep high layer with one-and-a-half-meter-thick concrete walls, and the hollow upper section contains an eight-meter-deep grid of concrete beams. The structure was abandoned before its completion and each of the incomplete but distinct sections left exposed to the outdoors developed its own microclimate. Clément took advantage of these microclimates to initiate the three gardens. The base layer of concrete was covered with a thin layer of four soil types—clay, sand, gravel, and large pebbles. He arranged the terrain in slopes and mounds and left it unplanted, allowing the ground to be seeded by wind, plants, and animals. Over the next five years, nearly 163 species came to occupy this zone, which he called the Garden of Labels. Clément envisaged the Garden of Stonecrops and Grasses on the second layer of the structure. Planting beds were positioned between existing concrete walls, taking advantage of the shaded areas. A soil mix consisting of rubble and sand was spread out, diversifying the terrain; species adaptable to dry and hostile environments were planted here. A thin water canal was added between the walls to irrigate the plants. Clément planted aspen trees in the hollow chambers of the top layer, naming it the Garden of Aspen Woods. These gardens demonstrate the capacity of ruins to host regional biodiversity. With little to no planting, the three gardens create a profusion of growth climates for many species. Clément limits the role of design to an initial transformation of the site, which facilitates the dynamic process of nature. Human intervention is an integral part of the ecology and the collaboration of humans and nonhumans influences the environmental equilibrium of the place.

Figure 1.2 Mixing room in the Patna opium factory, Lithograph, Walter Sherwill, c. 1850.

Figure 1.3 Opium factory repurposed as a thermal bath.

The central appeal of projects such as Clément's is that they observe and study the physical, material, and architectural qualities of ruins that let a rich biodiversity thrive. Because of limited human interaction and interference, ruins are more receptive to biological diversity than human-controlled and exploited urban areas. Reticent human activity lets other species exercise their agency to create habitats and assign functions to the space. Post-industrial urban areas have large precincts of abandoned and defunct factory buildings that have taken on the characteristics of ruins. Such sites embody the dominant politics and economics of the period in which they were constructed and are characterized by an architectural style and industrial function. Following their closure and subsequent abandonment, they linger for decades before a new use is assigned to them. The architect Ignasi de Solà-Morales Rubió used the term *terrain vague* to refer to such undefined parts of the city (Solà-Morales Rubió 1995). The unstructured nature of these spaces challenges imposed limits, orders, and forms (Mithal 2021, 145). As these ruins remain outside of and unrecognized by administrative systems, they become unpoliced spaces inviting opportunities for subversive expression, “blurring distinctions between practices deemed transgressive and rational” (Edensor 2005, 33). Ospedale al Mare in Italy is one such example which provides extensive vertical surfaces to artists for appropriation through graffiti.

Ruin Ecology: Medium for Decolonizing Histories

Industry is a product of modernization that led to urbanization and colonial oppression. A now neglected factory in the city of Patna was historically celebrated as marking the success of the British East India Company’s (EIC) opium business. Taking the example of this factory, Sonal Mithal’s studio “Ecotone: The Sentient Ruins” (2021) used 1850s archival colonial imagery to make artistic illustrations that reversed the colonizer–colonized relationship and presented the site as a space for multispecies collaborative habitats, as ruins that can reverse power dynamics. Using the available plans and elevations of the factory, students illustrated ways in which the building might transform, given the current ecological crisis, to survive the changed conditions. The following paragraphs provide a brief description of the opium factory and the artistic proposals from the studio.

In the late eighteenth century, the EIC built the factory in Patna to produce opium on an enormous scale, employing a thousand workers at the height of its business. The EIC forced Indians to work in the poppy fields, drying and mixing the milky fluid from poppy seeds to make opium balls. Each worker was expected to produce at least 100 opium balls per day. The balls were packed in timber chests and sent down the river to Calcutta to be exported. The military draftsman Walter Stanhope Sherwill produced a series of lithographs showing the examining hall, mixing room, balling room, drying room, and stacking room of the factory. These images show the Indian workers toiling under the watchful eye of the EIC Opium Agency managers. Opium production impoverished Indian peasants and triggered famine in the state of Bihar. After its abandonment, the Patna factory became a “ruin of the Empire” (Stoler 2008, 194) onto which a reverse gaze can be cast to reveal the colonial oppression of the people and land of the subcontinent.

Using Sherwill’s image of the mixing room **Fig 1.2**, the studio participant Roshita Sudhir imagined the opium factory repurposed as a thermal bath **Fig 1.3** to operate like Haraway’s terrapolis. Haraway writes that kin-making takes place in “risky embodied connections

Figure 1.4 **Bio-plastered wall allowing growth of halo-tolerant bacteria.**

Figure 1.5 Metal pipe system for desalination of water.

to places, corridors, histories, and ongoing decolonial and postcolonial struggles" (Haraway 2016b, 138). An attempt to decolonize India's history, the illustration recalibrates the kinship between plants and humans and investigates how the architecture, in the process, undergoes a metamorphosis to facilitate this collaboration. Poppy plants are interlaced with technology to act as thermostats that heat the water according to the temperature outside. The existing building envelope metamorphoses through decay and is gradually engulfed by a skin that mimics the thermoregulation mechanism in plants. The new skin responds to an increase in temperature or humidity by opening apertures, like stomata. The skeleton and membrane of the skin are made of natural polymer gel (referencing Neri Oxman's work at the MIT Media Lab). In addition to providing stiffness, the skeleton transmits electronic signals to the apertures distributed throughout the membrane. Equilibrium is essential for the sustenance of the terrapolis. The project attempted to subvert the racist, colonial, and capitalist nature of the opium factory through a reversal of the labor roles, showing the colonizer serving the colonized.

Another abandoned structure reminiscent of the modern world is the Ospedale al Mare on the Lido in Venice, Italy. It was established in 1868 as a tuberculosis treatment center offering alternative care such as heliotherapy and hydrotherapy. Since 2003, when the hospital was shut down, it has been a terrain vague, a site for squatters and subversive artistic expression. Discarded medical equipment, rooms, furniture, and the infrastructural remains of the hospital have been appropriated by artists to create sculptures, graffiti, and murals. In 2019, undergraduate students in Mithal's "Terrain-Vague Bricolage" studio reimagined the future of the redundant building to address the overbearing effects of climate change. They combined the characteristic properties of objects found at the Ospedale al Mare to imagine an entity that would increase the longevity of the building. The morphing of seemingly distinct entities into a unity referenced Haraway's cyborg. The studio participant Lisa Therese looked at the factors that led to the current state of the hospital, finding that prolonged exposure to saline has had a negative impact on the building: the sea breeze had eroded the walls and corroded the metal structural elements. She wondered if a layer that is adaptable to the saline atmosphere and can form its own system would help mitigate the problem. Studying halo-tolerance—the adaptation of living organisms to conditions of high salinity—she identified bacteria that thrive on higher salt concentrations. She proposed applying a mud plaster containing these bacteria to the walls. Exposure to saline and moisture would support the growth of the bacteria into mold. The bacterial strands would act differently according to the concentration of salt, moisture, and light, producing different colors on the wall over time, forming a natural graffiti. This bacterial mold could be cultivated from the walls and used to remove organic pollutants from water. Hence, the bio-plaster would form an adaptable wall **Fig 1.4**. The studio participant Riddhi Varma did not see the salt deposits as a problem, instead embracing them, channeling the process into a system that would allow salt to be extracted from the adjoining Adriatic Sea and deposited onto the walls using the air ducts already installed in the building. In turn, this process would reduce the salinity of the seawater around the island, decreasing the potential for damage to the foundation. The desalination would also allow new freshwater plant species to thrive, reshaping the ecology of the island and creating a completely new aesthetic for the building language and surrounding context **Fig 1.5**.

Taking an ecological approach to reading ruins is intertwined with acts of decolonizing history. The ruin aesthetic, an outcome of the European obsession with the pleasure and pathos of appreciating the innate beauty of the object of the ruin, privileges the colonial gaze. This colonial gaze has been instrumental in writing the architectural history of colonies such as India. Founded by the

British in 1861, the Archaeological Survey of India inventoried ruinous architectural objects, drawing them meticulously. British artists in the so-called Company School painted ruins in India for the delight of their European audiences—for example, Thomas Daniell's *Indian Landscape with Temple Ruins* (1820) Fig 1.6 and *Ruins of the Palace at Madura* (1785–94). To decolonize the local history, Mithal's "Staging Ecologies" studio, concerned with urban design interventions for the marginalized sections of society, undertook a mapping of queer spatial typologies, multispecies presence, expressions of decolonial memory, and subversive occupancy tactics at Qaiserbagh in Lucknow (Mithal 2023). Once a part of a glorious palace of Nawab Wajid Ali Shah, Qaiserbagh was destroyed by British colonizers following the 1857 War of Independence. Qaiserbagh put up resistance to British imperialism not only politically but also culturally. During the nawab's tenure (1846–56) Qaiserbagh was a site for theatrical performances which were choreographed by the nawab himself. These performances were undertaken daily and blurred the boundaries between the personal and the political life of the nawab. Housing people from intersectional identities of gender, sexuality, race, religion, and class, Qaiserbagh was theatrical and subverted the colonial gaze (Mithal and Paul 2024). Soon after its destruction, it was appropriated and transformed by the British into a clean, regimented precinct with geometric parks and gardens. Today, Qaiserbagh is a combination of colonial and nawabi[2] structures

2 Built during the reign of the nawabs. The nawabi period in Lucknow dated from the early 1700s to 1857.

Figure 1.6. Ruin aesthetic. "Indian Landscape with Temple Ruins" Oil on canvas, Thomas Daniell, 1820.

in various states of abandon. The studio participant Shivani Mehta mapped the ruination of the site. Following the geographer Tim Edensor's celebration of ruins as "other" spaces of disorder and Sanne Kanters's definition of ruination,[3] Mehta read Qaiserbagh as "a multiplication of possibilities [...] where that which usually gets banished from 'normal' urban life can flourish" (Minkjan 2016). She locates evidence of hybridity and human–nonhuman interdependencies in her mapping, which is a study of elevations of abandoned structures and their materials—a mix of both architectural and vegetal elements. The *lakhauri* bricks, or bricks used during the nawabi period, British bricks, present-day bricks, and plaster partially form the architectural materiality; moss, vegetation, roots, and debris that occupy the elevations partially form the nonhuman materiality. The mapping looks at these ma-

3 Kanters's definition appears in an interview with Mark Minkjan in the online journal *Failed Architecture*. The interview was about "celebrating otherness, alternatives to scripted cities and the promise of monsters". (Minkjan 2016).

Figure 1.7 Human–nonhuman interdependencies at Qaiserbagh in Lucknow, India.

terialities as hybrid outcomes of a ruination process. Through her drawings, Mehta shows that punctures in walls, niches, cracks, foliage, roots, soil debris, and ledges do not exist in isolation but rather work collectively as a system. Based on their relation with one another, she sees three systems emerging. First, *physical interactions,* where elements are directly in contact with one another, creating the highest level of hybridity—punctures, roots, niches, and vertical cracks are part of this system. Second, *proximal interactions,* where the proximity of one element to another leads to the creation of a hybrid—foliage and aerial roots are the main elements of this system. Third, *parasitic interactions,* where one element takes support from another, not in a symbiotic relationship like an actual hybrid but nevertheless contributing to the site ecology—soil debris on the wall, ledges, and horizontal

Figure 1.7 Human–nonhuman interdependencies at Qaiserbagh in Lucknow, India.

cracks contribute to this system Fig 1.7. These examples prompt us to think that buildings can be full of living components that strengthen and consolidate the structure with time. Whether in Dehradun or Qaiserbagh, a derelict building becomes a composite structure that stabilizes because of invading vegetation. These examples present ruins as sites of various alliances—multispecies and cyborgian. Building elements disintegrate, inviting vegetation to nestle in the debris. Vegetation catches traveling seeds, giving shape and space to unconventional and unfamiliar flora. Various participants contribute to this alliance, acknowledging one another's inequalities and requirements, working with contingent conditions of dirt and decay. Ruins offer a liberated field of companionship no longer controlled, sanitized, or inhibited by the burden of production for consumption.

2 From Feminist Ecologies to Architectural Thinking: Formulating a Vocabulary

To foster multispecies alliances, architecture needs to be freed of its determinism. Prioritizing the placement of an architectural object, architects begin with an analysis of the site, considering natural features such as topography, drainage, water runoff, presence of trees, ground cover and texture, and soil stability. Climatic conditions such as wind direction, sun path, rainfall, snowfall, humidity, and temperature are inventoried. Human-made features such as adjoining buildings, streets, roads, and sidewalks are noted along with ongoing human activities on the site and its surroundings. These parameters are useful to ensure stable building for human inhabitants. However, such an analysis does not acknowledge the presence of more-than-human species that get disturbed with the placement of the architectural object. It also fails to acknowledge that the more-than-human species reconfigure and reassemble creating new assemblages with the inserted architectural object. The object continues to disturb the environment with continuous emphasis on hygiene, sanitation, and maintenance; while the more-than-human environment continues to adapt and strives to thrive despite it. This capacity of the more-than-human environment to integrate the inserted architectural object has not had much attention in the architectural discourse. The absence of taking note of more-than-human components on the site has been one of the primary reasons for architecture's contribution to obscuration of multispecies from the environmental equation. Before architects even begin to design, it is important to imagine and set intentions for a place where these alliances could take place. A perspectival shift is needed in architecture before a design shift can follow and theories of feminist ecologies provide the necessary starting point.

As places of alliances that support multispecies collaborative survival, ruins offer a twofold lesson that can systematically be situated within architectural thinking and practice. First, the realization that ruins prioritize dirt over sterile conditions and foster hybrid over typology-based forms has the capacity to transform the architectural discourse of modernity. Second, the realization that physiological conditions such as fragility and vacancy become the drivers of the renewal and stability of the ruin leads us to understand that its vulnerability leads to its endurance. To bring this into architectural thinking, we have developed a new framework for reading and evaluating these ruins as more-than-human assemblages. The expansive scholarship on feminist ecologies has equipped us with nuanced observations of assemblages, but they have not been brought into architecture explicitly. Here, we will calibrate the properties of some of these concepts to make them architectural—that is, to translate them into spatial, material, and formal components. We turn toward Haraway's *terrapolis* and the concept of *assemblage* first defined by Gilles Deleuze and Félix Guattari and later, Manuel DeLanda. Then, we integrate Anna Tsing's *precarity*, Maurice Merleau-Ponty's *prise*, Mary Douglas's problematization of *purity as danger*, and Sara Ahmed's *inhabitance* to formulate a vocabulary of our own that is instrumental in deriving architectural acts. We propose that we need to treat all architectures as assemblages. We propose that a terrapolis and an assemblage display characteristics of *tentacularity*, *vacancy*, *hybridity*, *prosthetics*, *receptivity*, and *indeterminacy*.

Haraway proposes the terrapolis — an n-dimensional niche space inhabited by creatures from multiple species. It is a place for knotted patterns and possibilities. In the terrapolis, companion species engage in relentless processes of "becoming-with" a world in which "natures, cultures, subjects and objects do not preexist their intertwined worldings" (Haraway 2016b, 13)—that is, citizens of the terrapolis exist only in a state of codependency. In this understanding, humans are one of the codependent species, one whose presence is necessary to sustain other species. In mathematics, integral equations determine an unknown function through an addition of its numerous small parts. Haraway uses an integral equation to define terrapolis as a sum of *n* number of terra having *x* kinds of varying characteristics, including physis, capacity, sociality, and materiality, each with human and nonhuman participants (Haraway 2016b, 11). The lower limit of the equation, alpha, is ecological evolutionary developmental biology, which acknowledges that every aspect of the development of a species (human or nonhuman) is closely linked with its environment. Therefore, at the lowest limit of the terrapolis are numerous environments in which individual organisms grow and numerous worlds made up of individual organisms. In other words, it is a sum of numerous "worldings," or the making of worlds, that take place both simultaneously and across time. Anna Tsing helps unpack these multiple worldings, which she says overlap. Taking the examples of beavers, bacteria, plants, fungi, and humans, Tsing explains that all organisms continuously make "workable living arrangements" to survive, and in the process "each organism changes everyone's world" constantly (Tsing 2015, 22). No thing and no one evolves or exists independently of their surroundings. Human beings form just a very small component of such a large system. This integral equation frees the terrapolis from human exceptionalism.

The upper-limit omega is the condition where the pluriverse is recuperating. Here, omega is both a noun (pluriverse) and the adjective (recuperating) that describes it. Terrapolis is a world that acknowledges the ever-present capacity of the pluriverse to recuperate. The many worlds that form the lower limit are codependent on one another, forming a complex pluriverse. The pluriverse is perpetually seeking stability, a condition Haraway calls a state of constant recuperation. It is a compilation of diverse worlds and worldviews that challenge the modernist ontology of universalism in favor of the multiplicity of possible worlds. The pluriverse is a world where many worlds fit; it creates space for people to re-engage with the environment differently, in a meaningful and humble way. The terrapolis is a pluriversal space where the rights of humans and rights of nature are equally upheld. The ways toward a pluriverse are multiple, open, and in continuous evolution (Kothari et al. 2019, xvii–xxxv). By saying "recuperating terra's pluriverse," Haraway restates that such diverse worldviews have always existed in indigenous and local imaginations across the world and are often shunned by the modernist paradigm in favor of a universal goal for development (Haraway 2016b, 11).

Terrapolis exists in time, *t*, or worlding time. Worlding means to make worlds, to co-create worlds. Humans are not the only species that make worlds; numerous worlds are made, unmade, and remade by various nonhuman actors as well (Tsing 2015, 22). Therefore, the time needed for each of these worlds to emerge varies. These worlds do not follow the linear idea of time, nor do they all work at the same pace—moss works at a different speed and time than a creeper vine. Various species have various worlding times. Thus, the terrapolis is always in a state of making, never complete and ever contingent. Terrapolis is poly-temporal—that is, it spans generations.

A combination of *terra* (Greek for earth) and *polis* (Greek for city), terrapolis refers to a city for and of the earth to be inhabited by all species and bodies. It calls for more-than-human species to live where humans reside and humans to become part of ecological world-making projects. The embeddedness of architecture in the polis as a building project translates to a world-making process across times and generations, and is contingent on the survival conditions available. The architecture of a terrapolis is mutable, indeterminate, and ready for reworking.

Architecture can be freed of its determinism and longevity and visualized as an anatomy that emerges, mutates, and adapts with the changing context offered by the many times of worlding. The lower and upper limits of the terrapolis equation have an architectural mandate too. The terrapolis frees the architectural paradigm of human exceptionalism, calling for a need to "make living arrangements simultaneously for themselves and for others: multi-species worlds" (Tsing 2015, 22), facilitating the coexistence of different bodies, ideas, movements, and functions.

Similar to the terrapolis is the assemblage, which Deleuze and Guattari consider as a whole. Properties of the assemblage emerge from interactions among its parts. Within the assemblage, participants retain their properties and are available for "reciprocal presuppositions" and "mutual insertions" (Deleuze and Guattari 1985, 90)—that is, in the assemblage, actions and relationships among its multiple participants are always shared. An abandoned basalt quarry can be considered an assemblage of participating entities such as the broken basalt rock face and rock bed, tree roots, weeds, water, soil, wind, and gravity. Matter that makes a ruin is constantly in movement, relaying energy from one constituent to another. The tree roots interact with proximate fissures in the rock bed as they find their way down into the ground. Each participant exhibits an equal agency in the interaction. The rock bed loosens and recomposes itself around the root. Participants respond to available proximities in a variety of ways, which changes not only their characteristics but also the emergent assemblage. Tree roots may enfold loose rocks and consolidate the rock bed, which in turn becomes a receptor of eroding soil, which in turn becomes a breeding ground for new vegetation. Thus, the ruin assemblage keeps emerging.

A sedimentary rock is an assemblage of accumulation. Rock debris collected at the base of the quarry hill is in the process of consolidation, also an assemblage of accumulation. A fissure in a basalt rock that holds eroded soil and water is an assemblage of deduction. Manuel DeLanda treats heterogeneity as a variable of assemblage and not its constant property (DeLanda 2006, 11), thereby introducing a possibility of considering homogenous entities to also function as an assemblage. In this understanding, a tree is an assemblage too, and so is a fissure. An assemblage of accumulation or deduction is a "veritable invention" (Deleuze and Guattari 1985, 406). Such an assemblage is unique, real, and composed of elements that are selected, organized, and stratified through careful deduction from the flow of many elements. If we examine these processes literally and not metaphorically, as DeLanda proposes, then it is important to pay attention to factors such as the immediacy of the present elements, the speed at which elements move, and the directions the elements move; it is also important to pay attention to the capacity of the cavities and depths of the surrounding materials that will catch and hold them. These are just some of the many factors that lead to specific elements getting selected, the ways that the selected elements organize among themselves, and the characteristics of the resulting stratification. Every element can be broken down to its constituent capacities, such as its heat, sonority, density, tensility, malleability, and ductility, which determines its ability to respond to other constituents in an assemblage. Factors such as gravity, topography, force, and mass determine the flow of energy and matter.

Extending Deleuze and Guattari's definition of assemblage, DeLanda considers interpersonal networks and institutional organizations as assemblages of people and cities as assemblages of "conduits for matter and energy flows" (DeLanda 2006, 5–6). Individuals as bodies "oriented (physically or psychologically) towards each other" are participants in such social assemblages (DeLanda 2006, 12). He equates the sorting process to territorialization, in which homogenous groups begin to collate and segregate. Furthermore, he emphasizes that it is precisely when the boundaries of such territories become available for communication with other territories that deterritorialization takes place. Deterritorialization is important because it challenges exclusivity and homogeneous social groups; networks play a significant role in propelling it (DeLanda 2006, 13). DeLanda contends that social assemblages are composed of human bodies enmeshed with material participants ranging from food, labor, and tools to buildings and neighborhoods, forming intertwined networks (DeLanda 2006, 12). Architect Marco Casagrande's Treasure Hill in Taipei is an architectural example of assemblage similar to De Landa's model. It is an intervention that acknowledges and makes robust networks of people, infrastructure, amenities, and geography. An urban squatter settlement, Treasure Hill was planned to be demolished to make way for a park. Casagrande advocated against the demolition to instead propose minimal interventions that would consolidate the community residences on the hill. The project is discussed in more detail in Chapter 4.

Assemblage and terrapolis are characterized by tentacularity, hybridity, prosthetics, vacancy, receptivity, and indeterminacy, all of which are tangible and have architectural connotations. In the following paragraphs, we unpack each of these characteristics as they appear in ruins, and describe their architectural quality. Then, we provide an outline of mappable parameters for each characteristic, which can help read a ruin as an assemblage or a terrapolis.

54

Tentacularity

Participants in an assemblage are in a continuous state of movement, growing, adapting, and intertwining with other entities. It is their tentacular nature that facilitates this. Tentacles reach into available vacancies and grasp onto available opportunities to receive support for growth. They interweave with what they clutch. Their flexibility and adaptability lets them adjust and respond to components of the emergent assemblage. Tentacles know the assemblage through tactility. The surface of the tentacle has to be receptive for it to acknowledge changes in the proximate conditions of temperature, humidity, sound, and other sensory conditions. Tentacles are constantly navigating and exploring the assemblage. They can adhere to surfaces and maintain cohesion. Thus, they contribute to the creation and sustenance of the components of an assemblage. In a ruin, the roots of a tree are like tentacles that extend in directions made available to them by proximate elements. The tentacularity of the roots helps trees form connections and interact with other entities in the assemblage. To read a ruin as an assemblage is to read it for its participants and their tentacular properties and to identify the networks formed. Tentacularity is a material, tangible property of any element. Architecturally speaking, an element that can grasp, clutch, and reach out—and is linear, flexible, adaptable, and combines with available tectonic systems—is a tentacle. A beam or a ledge deriving its support from a cliff face is a tentacle. The service building of the Zinc Mine Museum designed by Peter Zumthor at the old Allmannajuvet mines in Sauda, Norway, can be read as a tentacle—supported by the cliff face, it hangs lightly over the Allmannajuvet landscape. To facilitate a multispecies habitat, it is imperative to imagine the tentacularity of architecture as a mechanism that not only seeks support from that which it latches onto but also initiates a support and thereby strengthens new networks.

Sara Ahmed directs our attention to the phenomenological ways in which various objects partake in a shared habitation of the world. Arguing that it is essentially a "bodily inhabitance" determined by orientation, Ahmed draws focus to the question of "who" or "what" we inhabit spaces with (Ahmed 2006, 1). Her scholarship on "queer phenomenology" is useful in reading ruins as a system of "bodily inhabitance" in which each participant directs their energy and attention toward proximate and not-so-proximate participants (Ahmed 2006, 3). In this inhabitance, each participant continuously reorients itself in response to the ever-changing availability of objects. This allows them to "deviate" from their "lines of existence" and forge new connections. Invoking Kant, Ahmed explains the "intercorporeal aspects of bodily dwelling": "Space then becomes a question of 'turning,' of directions taken, which not only allow things to appear, but also enable us to find our way through the world by situating ourselves in relation to such things" (Ahmed 2006, 5, 6).

Reading Ahmed, we argue that the sentient components know a ruin through their tactile senses, feeling proximate objects, impressing themselves onto those objects, and taking on the impressions of what touches them. Ahmed prioritizes "becoming familiar" over familiarity, which allows objects to be receptive to the objects around them. Despite the proximity, the objects will have to reach out to materialize their embodied knowledge (Ahmed 2006, 7). In the reaching out lies the tentacularity. Objects reach out, extend their bodies into space, and make the "strange familiar," creating "new folds" or "new contours" forming new semblances of occupations (Ahmed 2006, 11). Thus, the objects orient themselves in space and with this orientation the sentient components of a ruin have the agency to decide what to extend toward. Ahmed helps us spatialize how an object forms a tentacular relationship with others in order to strengthen its location, position, direction, and presence in the ruin. Prioritizing lines along which objects lie and lines that the bodily form of an object occupies in Ahmed's work, we argue that the sentient components of a ruin go in and out of reach of other objects, and this decides what tentacular actions a particular component can take. The components may move toward or away from other objects, and this further affects their actions. For example, in a ruin, ivy works like a tentacle by latching onto walls or other surfaces. Its tendrils grow by seeking out surfaces to attach to. They reach out and explore their surroundings, much like a tentacle seeking something to latch onto. When a tendril encounters a suitable surface, such as a wall, tree trunk, or another vertical structure, it coils around it. Equipped with specialized cells that can change shape and tighten, tendrils provide a firm grip on the surface. The tendrils make the unfamiliar familiar. Subsequently, they change the direction of the plant and help it climb, strengthening the plant's location, position, and direction. In the new direction, new objects become available to the plant. The plant's growth is aided by the tendrils, allowing it to reach new heights and access more sunlight. Over time, as the ivy continues to grow, more tendrils develop, latch onto nearby surfaces, and aid the plant's expansion. An ivy's tendrils work much like tentacles, as they actively reach out, attach to surfaces, and provide both support and a secure grip for the plant to climb and spread **Fig 2.1**. Jingkieng Jri, or Living Root Bridges, in the districts of West Jaintia Hills and East Khasi Hills in Meghalaya, India, are an example of tentacular architecture. Made from plant roots, these suspension bridges exemplify a traditional building system that acknowledges and modulates the intrinsic embodied tentacular knowledge of plants.

Figure 2.1 Roots displacing mortar and consolidating a brick wall at the abandoned Rajnagar Mills in Ahmedabad, India.

Hybridity

When participants of an assemblage interact with other entities, they change and sometimes fuse together to form hybrids—that is, new assemblages. A hybrid may be a fusing of biological and technological components, both organic and inorganic. Hybridity, which involves the merging of different elements, ensures richness and diversity within an assemblage. Hybridity makes the assemblage more resilient and capable of responding to dynamic environments. Haraway's cyborg, which disrupts established power structures, is a hybrid. In an assemblage, a hybrid acknowledges the agency of each participant, promoting equitable transactions. For the work *Portal* (2022) by the Australian artist Jamie North, two cylindrical columns were made out of cast concrete and industrial aggregates. These carefully crafted columns serve as an unexpected habitat for several plant species native to Brisbane. Nourished by water, indigenous plants established themselves in the crevices of the columns, forming a hybrid of plant and concrete—a resilient assemblage.

For Deleuze and Guattari, a rhizome is that which "becomes" using transversal communications and does not reproduce genealogically (Deleuze and Guattari 1985, 239). Foregrounding contagion, they argue that it is through "interkingdoms" and "unnatural participations" that "nature operates—against itself" (Deleuze and Guattari 1985, 242). Dismissing the conventional emphasis on "filiative production or hereditary reproduction, in which the only differences retained are a simple duality between sexes within the same species, and small modifications across generations," they emphasize the need to consider "many beings [coming] from different worlds [which] form rhizomes" (Deleuze and Guattari 1985, 242). The rhizome represents a multiplicity of interconnected elements cofunctioning by contagion and participating in assemblages. Furthermore, a rhizome is decentered—that is, it doesn't have a single point of origin or a privileged center (Deleuze and Guattari 1985, 8)—which challenges traditional notions of authority and control. A rhizome operates along lines passing "*between* things, *between* points," and hence encourages multiplicity by forming connections that expand an assemblage (Deleuze and Guattari 1985, 505).

A rewilding or ecological hybridization is prominent in architectural ruins left to decay for extended periods. Vegetation such as ivy and trees grows in and around the ruins, forming a hybrid of vegetation and architecture. Massive trees of the silk-cotton or strangler-fig varieties have taken root in the crevices of the walls and pavilions of temple ruins in Cambodia, especially Ta Prohm **Fig 2.2**. There are approximately 150 species in the temple complex, the most common of which is the sponge tree (*Tetrameles nudiflora*), which has taken over the temple structure. Its large gnarled pallet roots wind their way through the cracks and crevices, cling to the walls and loosen the lintels. Architect and archaeologist Maurice Glaize, who worked as a conservator in Angkor from 1937 to 1945, qualified the significance of preserving the vegetation along with the structure. Glaize admitted that his work at Ta Prohm was to "reconcile the creepers and the roots with the survival of the structure and the architecture" (Glaize 1993 [1944], 141). He identified various vegetation-architecture hybrids. He wrote about a sandstone and laterite gallery with a double row of columns toward its interior that was covered by a vault in the internal courtyard of the temple, whose structure was held together by the roots of a tree "growing on the vault itself which so appears to be suspended—held aloft by its grasping tentacles that hang to the ground like the limbs of a massive, slumbering beast" (Glaize 1993 [1944], 145). In another instance, Glaize observed what he called "a curious freak of nature;—a tree, having dislodged the stone pillars, has substituted instead one of its roots which supports the whole weight of the galleries architrave" (Glaize 1993 [1944], 147). In these structures, trees have taken the shape of the entrance, "enveloping each of its jamb stones in its roots with perfect symmetry" (Glaize 1993 [1944], 147). In holding the structure together, the tree forms a hybrid with the laterite and sandstone. The tree derives its strength from the underlying stone's ability to hold water, while the structure derives its stability from the roots of the tree it supports. The origin of the tree is not in the ground but on the surface of the structure—the roots follow the lines of the door jambs, the curves of the vault, and the shape of the pillars. It is a rhizome that has given rise to many more such multiplicities in the temple complex and has sustained a hybrid existence for almost a century after the archaeological conservation of the place began.

Deleuze and Guattari's definition of a rhizome helps us see the emergence of hybrid forms and materials in a ruin. Liberated sexually "not only from reproduction but also from genitality"

(Deleuze and Guattari 1985, 18), the rhizome forms hybrids through alliances wherever it is—"always in the middle, between things, interbeing, intermezzo" (Deleuze and Guattari 1985, 25). The interspecies collaborations that occur are essential for the vitality of the ruin and not the hereditary reproductive systems. Components of a ruin function as a prosthetic to other components, forming multiplicities and encouraging contagions for the ruin to expand and last. In acknowledging the quality of a rhizome, which operates by expansion, conquest, and offshoot, the prosthetic emerges (Deleuze and Guattari 1985, 21).

Figure 2.2 Hybrid relationship between the tree and the temple structure at Ta Prohm in Angkor Wat, Cambodia.

60

Prosthetics

A prosthesis, derived from the Greek *pro-* (instead of) and *thesis* (placing), is defined as the replacement of all or part of a damaged or diseased anatomical organ by an artificial device. A prosthesis is applied externally to support a fragile body. It is temporary in nature. Prosthetics is a branch of surgery concerned with the making and fitting of artificial body parts; hence, it is the act of mediation between an artificial device and the living body. Prostheses become relevant when the body has had an accident, undergone an amputation, or has weakened parts. In the wake of the ongoing destruction of species and relationships, Haraway argues that a terrapolis can only occur when the pluriverse recuperates. If that living body is a terrapolis or assemblage, an insert that helps in recuperating the pluriverse becomes a prosthesis. The prosthesis would ensure that the various individual environments of organisms occupying the lower limit of the terrapolis synchronize with one another and calibrate the necessary balance. Prosthetics are different from hybrids in their resistance to mutation. Medically speaking, the inserted prosthetic does not change as it supports the fragile body. Once the body has lived its life, the inserted prosthetics may appear as the remnant of a support system and become available to support something else. Prostheses such as bionic limbs become part of the body and complete otherwise broken or frail connections Fig 2.3. Prostheses such as cosmetic gloves, to cover myoelectric arms, can be removed or worn as and when needed. Prosthetics such as metal implants are recycled—titanium hips and cobalt-chrome knees are melted down and used in the construction of cars and planes, and sometimes sold for reuse in the medical industry. Within the decay, destruction, or decline of a ruin, transformative elements or mechanisms are the prostheses that compensate for a lack, enhance a feature, or adapt to the surroundings. Reading the terrapolis as a ruin, systems and architectures inserted into the body of the ruin become a

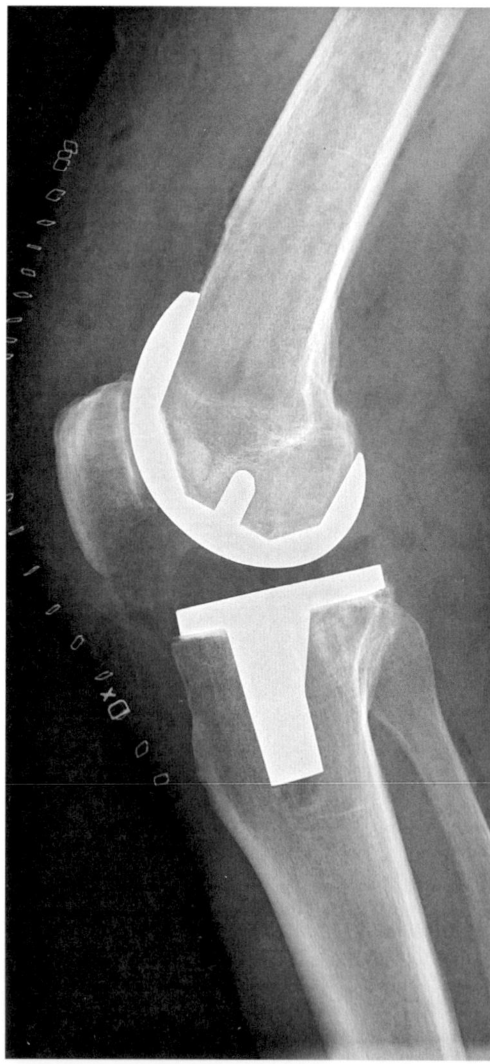

Figure 2.3 Lateral view of an X-ray of a knee prosthesis.

prosthesis. The prosthesis occupies available spaces in the vacancies of the host body, its purpose being to supplement a deficiency therein.

Vacancy

The components of an assemblage play a material and expressive role. The vibrancy of entities such as tree roots and the vacancy of a fractured rock collaborate and collude to stabilize the assemblage of the ruin—the hybrid that resists erosion. This is an example of territorialization in the ruin. The materiality of the tree roots helps it follow the available space in the cracked rock. Simultaneously, the materiality of the rock ensures the vacancy can hold moisture and soil as the tree root finds its way through it. The tree root is expressive in going in directions that are suitable to it; the vacancy is expressive in being accommodative. In the intermingling of the two entities, each reacting to the other, the assemblage of the ruin emerges.

At the top of a fractured basalt hill, the soil erodes further with each monsoon shower. The slopes of the hill are most susceptible to processes of deterritorialization. However, the eroding soil caught up in the fissures on the hill face keeps the hill stabilized, becoming part of the territorialization process. Here, the tree and the vacancy act as a rhizome—they are in a lateral relationship. The lines of the rhizome are what Deleuze and Guattari call *arborescence* (Deleuze and Guattari 1985, 34). When matter moves from one assemblage and into another, it deterritorializes the former and reterritorializes the latter. The example of the eroding soil is useful once again: The abandoned quarry is an assemblage consisting of a basalt hill, quarry pits, loose rocks, debris, denuded desire paths, caves, streams, forests, and heath. The basalt hill is an assemblage of several assemblages. The soil on the hilltop is part of the assemblage of the grassy terrain there, until it interacts with the rainwater that forcefully hits it, giving in to the gravity and weight of water. It leaves the assemblage of the terrain and enters the assemblage of flowing water. It remains part of that assemblage until it encounters a cavity in the rock and enacts its ability to cause friction to the moving water. The soil then enters the assemblage of the cavity and gets stabilized. It remains in that assemblage until other forms of matter start to collect there and change the composition and density of the accumulation.

The components of a ruin are constantly becoming an assemblage and an assemblage is constantly becoming, along with other components and other assemblages, a new assemblage. Reading an assemblage as the outcome of continuous deterritorializations and reterritorializations is to read it as a network of components and assemblages. The Vishwamitri River origi-

Figure 2.4 The meandering Vishwamitri River flowing through the agricultural fields in Gujarat, India.

nates in the hills of Pavagadh in the state of Gujarat and moves through the ruin of an abandoned basalt quarry, taking organic matter, leaves, seeds and fruits along with it—transporting them to other cities on its route before it combines with the Mahi and Narmada rivers, which drain into the Arabian Sea Fig 2.4. The water takes deterritorialized matter from Pavagadh and reterritorializes the agricultural regions in the watersheds of the two rivers. Similarly, the wind blows soil and seeds and migrating birds multiply the pollinating potential of the flora, reterritorializing the ruin. Thus, the movement of matter deterritorializes and reterritorializes the assemblage of the ruin. Ruins are outcomes of constant territorialization, deterritorialization, and reterritorialization because of a continuity of becoming-with processes. The inseparability of "assemblage haecceities and interassemblage haecceities" becomes visible in the heat, gravity, topography, and weight of the components, as well as the components themselves, such as roots, rocks, slopes, water, birds, and bees (Deleuze and Guattari 1985, 262). The components and the assemblage are inseparable—not unlike what Deleuze and Guattari call the inseparability of "climate, wind, season, hour [and] the things, animals, or people that populate them, follow them, sleep and awaken within them" (Deleuze and Guattari 1985, 263).

Receptivity

Phenomenologist Maurice Merleau-Ponty argued that "existing is being in and of the world," emphasizing embodiment, the lived body, perception as embodied action, and corporeal intentionality (Merleau-Ponty 2002 [1958], 421). The lived body (*le corps propre*) is the primary site of perception. Perception occurs because the body experiences things actively and makes connections based on its own corporeality. Tentacularity (discussed above) is a way to explain how there are things that reach out and there are things that can be grasped. Merleau-Ponty's *prise,* the "grip" of a perceiving body, contends that the grip itself is a function of a "connaturality" with other proximate perceiving bodies. In this emergent phenomenon of an ongoing becoming, the lived body directs its attention and intentions toward the world. Hence, the lived body is not a passive recipient of objective information or a passive response to external stimuli. Rather, it is active—its movements and the routes it takes form an integral part of its embodied perception. In this sense, the receptivity of the body that undertakes an embodied action in and of an assemblage is crucial. The body is simultaneously reaching out to and available for reciprocal connections. Extending Merleau-Ponty's philosophy to more-than-human participants of an assemblage helps us consider their embodied knowledge which materializes because they are in the assemblage. Similarly, an architectural body should be imagined and designed as continually responding and not a passive entity within a certain environment.

The elements of an assemblage perceive other elements because they are receptive to them, which is possible through a radicalization of corporeal senses. In her 2010 book *The Ethics of Earth Art*, art historian Amanda Boetzkes argues that receptivity is an artistic stance within the earth art movement that began in the 1960s to acknowledge that the earth is not a site that can be subjected to human signification, but is one that is only available to human senses, and can only be presented in its resistance to representation (Boetzkes 2010, 21). The earth artist's body is a receptive surface that reorients itself to the elemental earth. Receptivity privileges the encounter between the perceiving bodies of the earth and the artist rather than the representation of the former. Returning to the assemblage, the ruggedness, indentations, precipitousness, concavities, vacancies, crevices, niches, fractures, and cracks that form the corporeality of its constituents underscore its receptivity. Referring to Merleau-Ponty, we argue that the phenomenal bodies of the assemblage's constituents are receptive because they are "dynamically acquainted with each other" and their "receptors [...] so arranged [...] as to make possible, through their synergy, the perception of the object" (Merleau-Ponty 2002 [1958], 270).

Receptivity is responsiveness, or *response-ability* (Haraway 2016b, 2). It is an ability to direct attention, to orient and reorient, and to absorb. It combines an ability to be open and vulnerable, to accept, hold, and contain. Dirt as soil is receptive to bacteria, fungi, and the other microorganisms that inhabit it. It absorbs and retains water, receives and holds seeds, and receives roots when the seeds germinate. Soil is receptive to seeds. It is receptive to environmental change and adapts in response to weather patterns. In a ruin, vacancies such as cracks and irregular surfaces are receptive, having receptacles to receive and hold water, seeds, and soil.

The house sparrow (*Passer domesticus*) regularly takes dust baths in very fine soil as part of its preening to maintain the quality of its feathers **Fig 2.5**. It digs a shallow hole in the ground and flutters in it so the dust penetrates the feathers down to the skin. It then shakes the dust off, along with excess oil, parasites, and dead skin cells. The dust baths form a crucial role in the house sparrow's daily routine. An ornithological survey by the Indian Council of Agricultural Research revealed that coastal regions of India have seen a 70 to 80 percent decline in the population of house sparrows, while the states of Gujarat and Rajasthan have seen a decline of 20 percent in the last two decades (Sharma and Binner 2020, 1). The loss of soil surfaces in urban environments is one of the main reasons for this sudden decline. The creation of a healthy human habitat was one of the main goals of the modernist architectural approach, particularly in response to the widespread tuberculosis crisis at the time. Under this paradigm, the outside—soil and dust—was deemed unsanitary and sealed interiors were preferred. Modernist responses to urbanization also led to the paving of outdoor surfaces thereby creating a scarcity of spaces that allow sparrows to take dust baths. In her book *X-Ray Architecture* (2019), architectural historian Beatriz Colomina argues that modern architecture was shaped by the dominant medical obsession of its time, tuberculosis, and the technology that became associated with it, namely the X-ray (Colomina 2019, 10). Until the exact causes of tuberculosis were found, hygiene and clean surfaces were viewed as preventive measures if not a cure. Here, modern architecture solidifies its ideal of eradicating all forms of dirt for clean,

Figure 2.5 House sparrow foraging for food in a dry grassy landscape.

white, hygienic spaces. This obsession with cleanliness, whiteness, and smoothness went beyond the design ideal of health to become a modern aesthetic, which in the aftermath of World War I also represented calm, and continued until the present time. To have a clean space means eradicating all undesired matter and species from the environment, making the built environment increasingly hostile to the growth and proliferation of other plant, insect, and animal species.

Contrary to the modernist wish to erase any kind of dirt, Mary Douglas, in her 1966 book *Purity and Danger*, calls for the need to reflect on this perspective: "There is no such thing as absolute dirt: it exists in the eye of the beholder" (Douglas 1966, 2). She argues that dirt is a relative concept; dirt in one place may not be dirt in another (Douglas 1966, 44). Citing cultures in which eating with one's hands is the norm as well as cultures that employ cutlery to not get their hands "dirty," she points out that cultures define dirt differently. Such a relative understanding plays a key role in imagining cohabitative survival, allowing us to see plural uses of one material and move toward more entangled human and more-than-human worldly relations (Frichot 2019, 17).

Dirt is receptive. As seen in the case of the house sparrow, soil sticks to the surface of the feathers, absorbing oils. Soil is receptive to grease and parasites that could inhibit the sparrow's capacity to fly. Clean and smooth surfaces do not have a receptive quality. The garden in the modernist project is a highly manicured landscape, presented in its usefulness for the human resident, not as a naturally proliferating space. Colomina explains how Le Corbusier prioritized using pilotis (thin columns) to detach the house from the "wet, humid ground, where disease breeds," and using the roof as a garden for sunbathing and exercise (Colomina 2019, 20). In Corbusier's concept of "exact air," the outdoor air is continually circulated and cleaned, made "dust free, disinfected [...] and ready to be consumed by the lung" (Colomina 2019, 22). Colomina argues that the building elements that prioritized human health were mainstreamed—particularly the pilotis, roof gardens, glass walls, and clean air—and became essential to modern architecture, as they were considered medical devices and extended the environment of a sanatorium devoted to preventive and reactive cures (Colomina 2019, 22). Colomina's argument helps us to understand the conditions under which modern architecture became exclusive to the service of the human. For example, the primary purpose of the roof garden in Corbusier's Villa Stein, in Vaucresson, a city west of Paris, is meant solely for exercise and sunbathing in order to maintain a healthy body (Colomina 2019, 22). Contained within planters, the plants and soils lose their functionality in the larger ecosystem. The plants become detached from the possibility of encountering and connecting with other plants. The soil in the planter bed is deprived of any possibility of hosting new plants other than the ones planted in it. Smooth, white, sterile surfaces and spaces don't have the capacity to host life. Contamination makes diversity (Tsing 2015, 29), and getting messy with other earthly beings, or *messmates* (Haraway 2016b, 170), is key in forging relationships with other species. Appropriation takes place through dirt (Serres 2011, 3); in its absence, there is a lack of matter available for more-than-human species to inhabit.

Indeterminacy

Terrapolis demands deliberate human disturbance. One such example is provided by Anna Tsing, when she cites Kato-san disagreeing with her observation that forests can restore themselves best on their own: "If you want matsutake in Japan, you must have pine, and if you want pine, you must have human disturbance" (Tsing 2015, 151). With the example of matsutake, Tsing emphasizes that human disturbance is a necessary condition to initiate possibilities for transformative encounter (Tsing 2015, 152). Matsutake mushrooms (*Tricholoma matsutake*) grow on red pine trees (*Pinus densiflora*), which need sunlight and the minerals in the soil left by human deforestation. If forests are allowed to grow back without human disturbance, broadleaf trees will obstruct the pines, which would stop germinating along with the matsutake (Tsing 2015, 6). However, matsutake have the ability to nurture trees and help forests grow in daunting places, participating in collaborative survival (Tsing 2015, 4), with disturbance as an essential component. Tsing rejects the humanist version of disturbance that considers it synonymous with damage and instead provides an explanation of how disturbance renews ecologies and opens up possibilities for "transformative encounters, making new landscape assemblages possible" (Tsing 2015, 160). Such encounters, emerging from disturbance, lead to contamination. Contamination changes those who participate in the encounter, thus changing "world-making projects, mutual worlds" (Tsing 2015, 27). Such encounters are not planned and cannot be planned; they rely on precarity. Giving the example of matsutake mushroom pickers, Tsing insists on the importance of precarity. Since the uncertain conditions of the forest do not let the pickers plan their work, this precarity necessitates them taking notice of what is available. Calling for a need to acknowledge the centrality of precarity to ecological systems, Tsing emphasizes the ubiquity of precarity, which is a constant condition of our times, not an exceptional glitch (Tsing 2015, 20). Precarity, in Tsing's framework, refers to a condition of uncertainty, vulnerability, and instability experienced by various actors—human and nonhuman—as they participate in shaping one another's fates. Ruins can be considered "sites for more-than-human dramas, [...] radical tools for decentering human hubris. [...] Not backdrops for historical action, they are themselves active. Watching landscapes in formation shows humans joining other living beings in shaping worlds" (Tsing 2015, 152). Ruins emerge from disturbance, where precarity is enacted in more-than-human sociality.

In this configuration, humans are dependent on the actions of more-than-humans. The architect's obsession with planning misses opportunities to notice precarious situations. Thinking through precarity can help architecture revisit its obsession with deterministic forms. Architecture can limit itself to creating conditions for habitations that can be fully realized by those who inhabit them; thus, architecture would be open to adaptation. Precarity challenges architecture's obsession with controlling form, which is driven by modernist ideals of defined aesthetics and monumentality. It can help architects share control for the creation of habitats with other-than-humans; it also helps architects notice what and whom is available to work with. Such unpredictable encounters are transformative, letting an architect lose control and become vulnerable. This vulnerability allows for continuous interaction, awareness of the environment, and an ability to continuously transform and adapt our structures.

Meret Oppenheim Turmbrunnen (1983), a fountain in Bern, Switzerland, by Surrealist artist Meret Oppenheim, is an example of indeterminate architecture **Fig 2.6**. It demonstrates a continuously transforming relationship between vegetative growth, water, and concrete. Two spirals run around a column's surface: one carrying water, the other supporting plants. An unforeseen amount of calcium deposits, from the high chalk content of the water, keep forming on the concrete. These deposits, along with vegetation such as grass, moss, and even tree saplings, have turned the fountain into a continuously transforming biotope. Out of the 49

Figure 2.6 Meret Oppenheim Turmbrunnen, Bern, Switzerland

species planted when the fountain was built, 16 have survived while 10 unplanted species were discovered a few years later. The indeterminacy and loss of control over the visual aesthetic of the fountain made this growth possible. In 2007, Heinz Isler, the structural engineer for the project, calculated that the plant growth did not threaten the strength of the structure.[1] The human participates in this multispecies growth through periodic cleaning of the mineral deposits and plants. This cleaning is a disturbance that keeps making space for new deposits, and hence support for existing and new plant species.

Indeterminacy makes life possible. Ruins allow growth by losing determinacy. The question of how a building should age may not be completely in the hands of an architect. Indeterminacy makes unusual and unforeseen encounters that lead to unusual and unforeseen connections. These may be hybrid materials and hybrid forms that are more resilient, adaptive to change, and accommodate more habitations. Thus, buildings do not and need not look the same over time. Architects can let go of their fixation on keeping buildings look like they never change.

Tentacularity can be observed in the physical characteristics of inhabiting species and the physical characteristics of their immediate environments, which provide support to the tentacles. Mapping the species that proliferate in the ruin, and the surfaces and crevices they latch onto and crawl into, helps us see how tentacularity emerges. To perceive it is to keenly observe the interdependencies of species with their surroundings for growth and food. Tentacularity is dependent on the irregularity of proximate surfaces as well as temperature and moisture. Mapping interdependencies reveals direct and indirect relations among species, materials, and environments enmeshed with one another, forming networks. Mapping these relationships leads to the mapping of networks. Nothing and no one operates in isolation; everything operates within networks of multiple scales. Processes of disintegration, decay, and erosion create spaces for new materials to leave deposits and consolidate the unstable system, eventually leading to hybrid systems. In the ruin, these hybrid systems are conducive for species growth. Looking at disintegration processes and following the outcomes leads to the mapping of hybridity. Resulting from disintegration and decay, vacancies give rise to spatial systems of different scales to be inhabited by various species of plants, rodents, birds, and other animals. Mapping vacancies allows us to see these spatial systems appropriated as habitats by other species. Vacancies also pro-

1 The work of Meret Openheim and the fountain in Bern was first introduced to us by Prof Sarah Nichols (THEMA, EPFL) in 2024. This example along with other works of Heinz Isler was part of the exhibit "Concrete: Cosmetic and Care", THEMA contribution to The Great Repair exhibition in Berlin, 14 October 2023–14 January 2024.

vide opportunities for placing prosthetics to initiate renewal and strengthening processes. Prosthetics can increase the functionality of the ruin in allowing other species to grow and spread. To let something attach to oneself is a condition of receptivity. There are two ways of mapping receptivity—first, through materiality, and second, through spatiality. Dirt is an example of the materiality of ruins. As discussed above, dirt is receptive in its capacity to hold life. Irregular surfaces, crevices, and vacancies are spatial receptors. The indeterminacy and precarity of a ruin are partially dependent on human disturbance. Mapping instances of what has conventionally been termed vandalism in abandoned spaces allows us to read the indeterminacy and precarity of ruins.

Ruins are a terrapolis, constituting assemblages of myriad species and living systems. Ruins offer conditions conducive to these systems, encouraging capacities for tentacularity, receptivity, and pre-carity, forging networks and forming hybrid systems. Ruins are sentient—response-able toward life-forms and their immediate and interdependent requirements for growth and sustenance. We propose Mapping Sentience in ruins as a method to derive architectural lessons in reading and responding to multispecies relationships. To become response-able to more-than-human life-forms, architecture has to be reimagined like a terrapolis. Equating the terrapolis characteristics of ruins to architecture, Mapping Sentience will give us parameters for identifying material and spatial conditions that can be created, and for revisiting design decisions to make architecture inclusive of a variety of life-forms.

3 Mapping the Sentient Ruin

Sentience originates from the Latin *sentire* (to feel). It describes an ability to feel, perceive, and show awareness of and respond to one's surroundings. Sentience equates to being alive.

Water runs through the cracks in a disused basalt quarry, carrying loose soil. The loose soil finds a safe spot to accumulate in the microscopic crevices in the porphyritic rocks, while the water leaks out of the cracks and down the face of the hill. Fungus finds an ambient condition there to thrive and, in turn, invites insects. At abandoned mills, the thick brick walls disintegrate with time. In the process, they make spaces where plant and tree species can latch onto newly available surfaces and rodent and bird species can nest within. The ruination of the site, both in time and scale, creates a system of relationships among organic and inorganic elements—ongoing, open-ended interdependencies owing to proximity. These interdependencies make ruins sentient. Forever changing, ruins allow for a sustained condition for resilience and survival through adaptation, leading to new conditions that involve new actors.

Mapping Sentience looks for the existing and emerging conditions that enable and sustain these interdependencies, combining scientific and phenomenological methods to find material indicators of nonhuman agents. These agents are persistently in a state of identifying and sustaining interdependencies for their own survival. Mapping Sentience spatializes and identifies the proximities of the elements involved while not being limited to quantifying them.

What Is Mapping Sentience?

Following Gilles Deleuze and Félix Guattari (1985), Mapping Sentience charts assemblages—entities, territories, and processes of reterritorialization and deterritorialization. Mapping Sentience combines embodied navigation, quantifying and spatializing elements, and affective forces as well as tracing mutual relationships. An embodied navigation through the assemblage is a participation in the assemblage, allowing oneself to be available—and hence vulnerable—to the forces at play, to explore in proximity, to become, and to locate through empathy. This navigation relies on minimizing the distance between the one who maps and that which is being mapped, making the discreet multispecies assemblages visible. Moreover, Mapping Sentience situates and reveals conditions that make the occurrence of these assemblages possible through scientific objectivity.

Landscape architect and theorist James Corner echoes Deleuze and Guattari's call to "make a map not a tracing" (Corner 1999, 214). Instead of outlining an objectively definable site, Corner looks for an active milieu—a field of connections, relationships, extensions, and potential (Corner 1999, 224). A ruin is a milieu that multispecies critters inhabit. It is a terrapolis, whose citizens exist in a state of intertwined codependencies. Here, humans are only one of the many codependent species—one whose presence is necessary to sustain other species. Mapping is an act of participation in the terrapolis. Corner provides frameworks for mappings that reveal the otherwise hidden and inaccessible entities, identify and rework polyvalent conditions, and make sense of the ever-emerging milieu. While surprised by the lack of scholarly progress and mapping innovations—despite the emergence of new theories in design and planning—he identifies four contemporary practices of mapping that have prompted shifts in design practice: first, the drift (inspired by Situationist dérive), which involves an unplanned, experience-based journey through an urban landscape where the participant is led by the terrain and the encounters therein; second, layering, which is the superimposition of various independent layers of information to produce a heterogeneous thickened surface; third, gameboard map structures, with working surfaces where competing constituencies are invited to negotiate; and fourth, the rhizome, which is an inclusive process of disclosure and enablement that acknowledges multiple nonhierarchical representations and interpretations and subverts reductive mapping strategies (Corner 1999, 231–50). Corner's scholarship offers a method to look for relationships among various factors in a milieu and not map objects in isolation at a static site in order to treat the milieu as a site with its own agency—cultural, ecological, social. Focusing on the ecological agency of the milieu, Mapping Sentience is similar to Corner's layering and rhizome practices—open, connectable "experimentations with the real" (Corner 1999, 244). An embodied navigation undertaken through the body of the mapper acknowledges the way the moving body perceives the milieu, creating a new knowledge of the milieu. It participates in and furthers the "becoming" of the assemblage. Through layering, Mapping Sentience offers a synthesis of multiple parts and elements; when layers are seen together, new possibilities of emerging assemblages become visible. In these new possibilities, the ruins reveal their sentience. For Corner, mapping's agency is "most effective when its capacity for description also sets the conditions for new eidetic and physical worlds to emerge" (Corner 1999, 214). This is what Mapping Sentience attempts to embody and demonstrate.

Mapping Sentience Is Embodied

Philosopher Edward Casey, in *Earth-Mapping: Artists Reshaping Landscape* (2005), illustrates various mapping techniques used by artists to explore humans' relationship to earth, place, and space. Rejecting the post-Renaissance maps as disconnected from earth (their subject), Casey proposes a way of mapping where the map itself becomes an earth art. This method situates itself on the earth's surface, combining various features of the planet in its making instead of just representing them from a far-off distance. Casey reduces the distance between the observer and the mapped while mapping the earth and the various interrelations of its elements. The enhanced proximity helps create an experiential rather than a Cartesian map, which relies on distance from the subject. Defying the Cartesian method of mapping, Casey makes a case for *going through* the land (Casey 2005, xv). For him, mapping is "the kind of intimate touching and close-up looking that occurs between parent and infant, between lovers, and between humans and certain animals. In these experiences, looking and touching merge in and on the body surface" (Casey 2005, xvii). Such a mapping treats the earth as a living body and a proximate subject of the one who maps. The mapper "travels intensely, not merely extensively, over the body of the earth" (Casey 2005, xvii). Drawing on Casey, Mapping Sentience emphasizes the need for a phenomenological navigation of the territory. In this embodied navigation, the person who maps makes explicit their own cognition of hostile elements on the site, their bodily effort to move through the topography, and the encounters that make certain routes available to them. While the human body allows itself to be led by what is on the site and follows those directions, it is also aware of and concerned for its own safety. Thus, it traverses the environment while looking for—in order to avoid—hostile elements. Taking advantage of the embodied navigation of the site, Mapping Sentience pays attention to those seemingly hostile elements to see how they appropriate the environment and forge dependencies—parasitic or mutual—for the benefit of their own survival. Mapping Sentience becomes an act of emulation and empathy. Its process allows one to empathize with the nonhuman actors on the site, and through that empathy one cultivates the ability to be more attentive to the various interdependencies at play. Mapping Sentience follows the routes taken by nonhuman elements—changing and aligning with directions when encountering new conditions. Thus, it is open-ended and unpredictable, relying on encounters. It emphasizes "paying at tention and noticing" (Tsing 2015, 37) the nuances of life-forms that allow humans to read, participate in, and respond to multispecies relationships and assemblages. It is about paying attention to nonhuman elements and their proximate encounters with others as they navigate the territory. This aspect of paying attention is essentially a result of the embodied experience of being in and of the assemblage. It is a subversion of mapping limited to documentation and recording.

The challenge with phenomenological navigation is sharing it. To share, and more importantly, to devise tools of translating the experiential into the measurable, Mapping Sentience draws on landscape architect Ian McHarg's method of layering. In *Design with Nature* (1969), McHarg illustrates a method of site analysis that layers several transparent maps. Each layer represents social factors as they coincide with varying environmental factors. Like the present-day data intensive Geographic Information System–driven site analysis, McHarg's mapping strategy prepares composite drawings to reveal the most suitable set of conditions for development. His pioneering work combined ecological and physiographic information such as land qualities, geological and soil features, and vegetation types with the suitability of human activity and settlement. McHarg's maps were one of the first examples of layering datasets visually to understand and reveal how different land conditions might affect one another. McHarg layered manually printed transparent color maps, as the technology available at the time allowed. His work has acquired a prescriptive reputation owing to its ability to provide designers with methods for effective problem solving. The rationality of this objective quantification model can be contested in favor of more inclusive and open-ended representation in mapping processes. However, an embodied navigation that participates in the making of the assemblage is limited in its capacity to identify the physical patterns that make these assemblages possible. Hence, an embodied participation combined with a scientific reading is necessary. The following sections of this chapter show the method developed in Mapping Sentience. Atmospheric conditions such as altitude, moisture, wind, gravity, sunlight, and heat, combined with physical conditions such as protrusions, undulations, and voids are mapped as layers superimposed with the evidence of existing life-forms such as moss, birds, and squirrels. Combining strategies of embodied navigation, rhizomatic discoveries, and layering, Mapping Sentience reveals a ruin's response-ability in accommodating varied life-forms.

To demonstrate Mapping Sentience, we follow the ruins at three post-industrial sites: two abandoned textile mills in Ahmedabad and the abandoned basalt quarries in Champaner—all in Gujarat, India. The first two are urban sites whose ownership is being contested, and the latter is a peri-urban site that has outlived its capacity to mine basalt. The first mill in Ahmedabad was established in 1861 and by 1939 there were 77 mills in the city. Due to the changing economy, mills started to slowly shut down and by 1996, almost all the mills had been locked down (Mithal and Khanwalkar 2018, 324–25). The New Commercial Mill (NC Mill) is located in the Amdapura area, northeast of the walled city of Ahmedabad, and is surrounded by industrial complexes. Spread across 1,610 square meters, this largely forested area houses three dilapidated mill structures. The site is used by the neighboring residents as a thoroughfare. Some of the site is inhabited by factory workers and women employed as domestic help nearby.

The Pickers Mill is a ruinous erstwhile production facility for leather pickers, workers whose job was to propel the weft-carrying element (shuttle) along the correct trajectory in textile machines. When the mill closed, the workers were promised 20 percent of the mill land for housing, which has yet to be granted (Mithal and Khanwalkar 2018, 328). By ensuring a hostile environment to keep people away, the workers found a way to ensure their stake in the land. The site is surrounded by slums where the former workers live. They use the mill's open spaces for informal gatherings, to play cricket, and for gambling. The number of discarded playing cards and plastic cups (apparently used to consume alcohol in an otherwise prohibitionist state) are testimony to the gambling and drinking activities that go on here. One may dismiss these as antisocial activities on an abandoned site, but they are a strategic tool to guard the workers' property rights.

The abandoned basalt quarry in the UNESCO World Heritage site of Champaner-Pavagadh Archaeological Park in Gujarat contains materials that are instrumental to its recovery. There are approximately 71 abandoned quarries spread across an area of 102 hectares of forest land and 94 hectares of revenue land (for agriculture) in Champaner. Following public interest, litigation citing river pollution, and damages to the forest, the quarries stopped functioning in the 1990s. The 2004 World Heritage site designation, as well as the unique basalt, rhyolite, and sandstone geology, flora, fauna, water sources, topography, and historical structures, make it an ecologically sensitive zone. Technological heritage, cultural heritage, and environmental heritage are intertwined on this site to create a multispecies landscape that requires innovative strategies for sustainability.

Mapping Sentience has two components: Mapping Interdependencies and Persistent Queering. Mapping Interdependencies within assemblages illustrates how the ruins are receptive to nature. It looks for the conditions that sustain life and lead to new and emerging possibilities for life-forms. It illustrates how conditions of distress are conducive for interdependencies to take shape, such as surface irregularity, vandalism, disintegration, hybridity, and spatial vacancies, combined with atmospheric conditions such as temperature, moisture, and gravity. As the mapping body navigates the assemblage, it enters into one coalition and leaves others. It continuously deterritorializes and reterritorializes, altering the assemblage. Similarly, the constituent elements of an assemblage (inter)act with and among one another, altering one another as well as the assemblage. The assemblages are hybrids of elemental entities that are continuously changing and adapting, forming new hybrids. These new hybrids, in turn, adapt to human presence as well as built and unbuilt conditions. In other words, they adapt to the sentience available, disrupting their existing composition, and entering into new alliances—forming a new assemblage. This way the assemblage is in a state of Persistent Queering, of which Mapping Sentience is cognizant.

Mapping Interdependencies

Mapping Interdependencies is concerned with interrelations among the nonhuman agents and the built forms on the site. Interdependencies are (inter)actions or actions where two (or more) entities affect each other. Mapping Sentience shows the (inter) actions between the human-built environments and nonhumans. The built form of the mill was not designed to harbor these interdependencies, but over time it was appropriated by the various nonhuman agents living on the site to facilitate their own proliferation. Mapping Interdependencies locates the qualities of the abandoned built form that allow for nonhuman species such as squirrels, lizards, and birds to proliferate on and around the structure. Through the participation of the abandoned structure in cohabitative survival, the mills and quarries become unique sites of study of how architecture can be made "response-able" toward more-than-human species.

The first step of mapping is navigating the site to become aware of and distance oneself from things that are uncomfortable to the human body. In that discomfort, one navigates the milieu in a proximate encounter with the other-than-human species that thrive there. This embodied human movement is invasive. Discussing the Pigeon Loft project in Melbourne's Batman Park, an example of response-able built form, Donna Haraway opines that the project is not pro-life since no serious human–nonhuman collaboration can be completely pro-life (Haraway 2016, 28). Built over an industrial wasteland, the loft is a hatching control system where the pigeons are provided space for roosting and the eggs are replaced with artificial eggs from below to brood. As the only feeding spot for pigeons in the region, it attracts many of the birds from the surrounding urban areas. Haraway sees the Pigeon Loft "as a small, practical enactment and a reminder to further opening to the response-ability of staying with the trouble. Response-ability is about both absence and presence, killing and nurturing, living and dying—and remembering who lives and who dies" (Haraway 2016, 28). In a similar vein, embodied navigation is a violent act. Such projects do not strive to undo natural inequalities but are attempts to get along with other species in a complex ecological web.

Interdependencies at the New Commercial Mill

As we undertake an embodied navigation of the NC Mill, we are primarily guided by the existing walls of the dilapidated structure. The walls provide a direction to follow, orienting the human body, and simultaneously offering a sense of enclosure and the familiar tactility of bricks. The body is continuously aligning and realigning itself along the length of the wall, observing the proximate objects it encounters in orthogonal directions. Lying unattended since 2012, the ruinous wall appears as a palette of diverse textures. Colors such as yellow and red combine with the dry crumbly granularity in some places, coats of blue paint combine with smooth plasters and green gooey moss at others. Palms of hands feel cold dampness in shaded places and cannot bear the touch of the hot surface at others. Indentations are almost as deep as the thickness of the wall, sometimes half-a-brick deep, sometimes just a dent, and sometimes wall cavities seem to be caused by human vandalism.

The crumbling material and eroding surfaces have become shelters for the Indian palm squirrel (*Funambulus palmarum*), lizards (*Hemidactylus frenatus*), and rats (*Rattus rattus*). Touching the wall, the body registers the smallest change in textures, depth of ruination, dampness, and surface temperature. Birds rest in the niches that have formed in the decaying wall surface, while squirrels scamper and stash their food supply in parts of the broken wall. The dampness and paucity of direct sunshine encourage the growth of algae and moss. Embodied navigation turns to these organicities. It navigates the height of the wall to trace the spread of moss, taking note of the spread of dampness. It navigates the length of the wall to trace the squirrel's route to and from its source of food, taking note of the spread and the continuity of the indentations in the wall surface. It takes note of a vacancy that offers itself as an opportunity for another life-form, such as a squirrel or lizard, to take over and rehabilitate it. Often, trees intercept the embodied walk and the body realigns itself to pause and acclimate to a slight drop in temperature from the light filering in through the foliage. A squirrel runs along a branch that connects to a depression in the wall. Partially owing to the crumbling brick and the force of the growing tree, the depressions become pronounced, which the squirrel takes advantage of. The embodied navigation circumvents the girth of the tree trunk and continues to move along the wall, searching for that which makes the mill a ruin—a place that harbors multispecies habitation, an assemblage.

Moving toward the wall, the primary observations are visual and map the presence and absence of elements on the wall's surface. The movement is obstructed by trees growing against the wall, which leads to a reorientation toward the tree, its branches, foliage, and relation to the built form. Visually tracing the branches reaching the roof of the mill and breaking through it leads to the discovery of various squirrel paths and hence the interdependencies that the condition creates. The shade created by the foliage makes the upper half of the wall damper and more receptive to moss growth. The surroundings are extensively traced through both visual sense and bodily movement.

The embodied navigation is accompanied by a heightened awareness of the surroundings. The absence of humans, the overwhelming nonhuman presence, and a general discomfort at seeing the evidence of human civilization in a state of deterioration make the body feel unfamiliar. In this state of heightened awareness, the body adapts to its surroundings, comprehending it; hence, the body becomes *familiar* (Ahmed 2006, 86). By paying attention to what it deems hostile, the body becomes empathetic to other life-forms and interdependencies. The body learns that the ruin has become a necessary condition for inaugurating interdependency. The ruin is conducive to interdependency through two conditions: that of temperature variation and moisture as well as that of surface irregularity.

Conducive Condition of Temperature Variation and Moisture

This first condition causes vegetal growth to permeate the ruin. On the east-facing wall, which forms the front of the mill, fresh and wet green moss grows on the upper part. **Fig 3.1a** The growth of moss is marked in green. Rainwater that has seeped into the walls does not evaporate owing to the

Figure 3.1 Effect of temperature and moisture on the vegetal growth on the east-facing (a), south-facing (b), and west-facing (c) facades of the NC Mill in Ahmedabad, India.

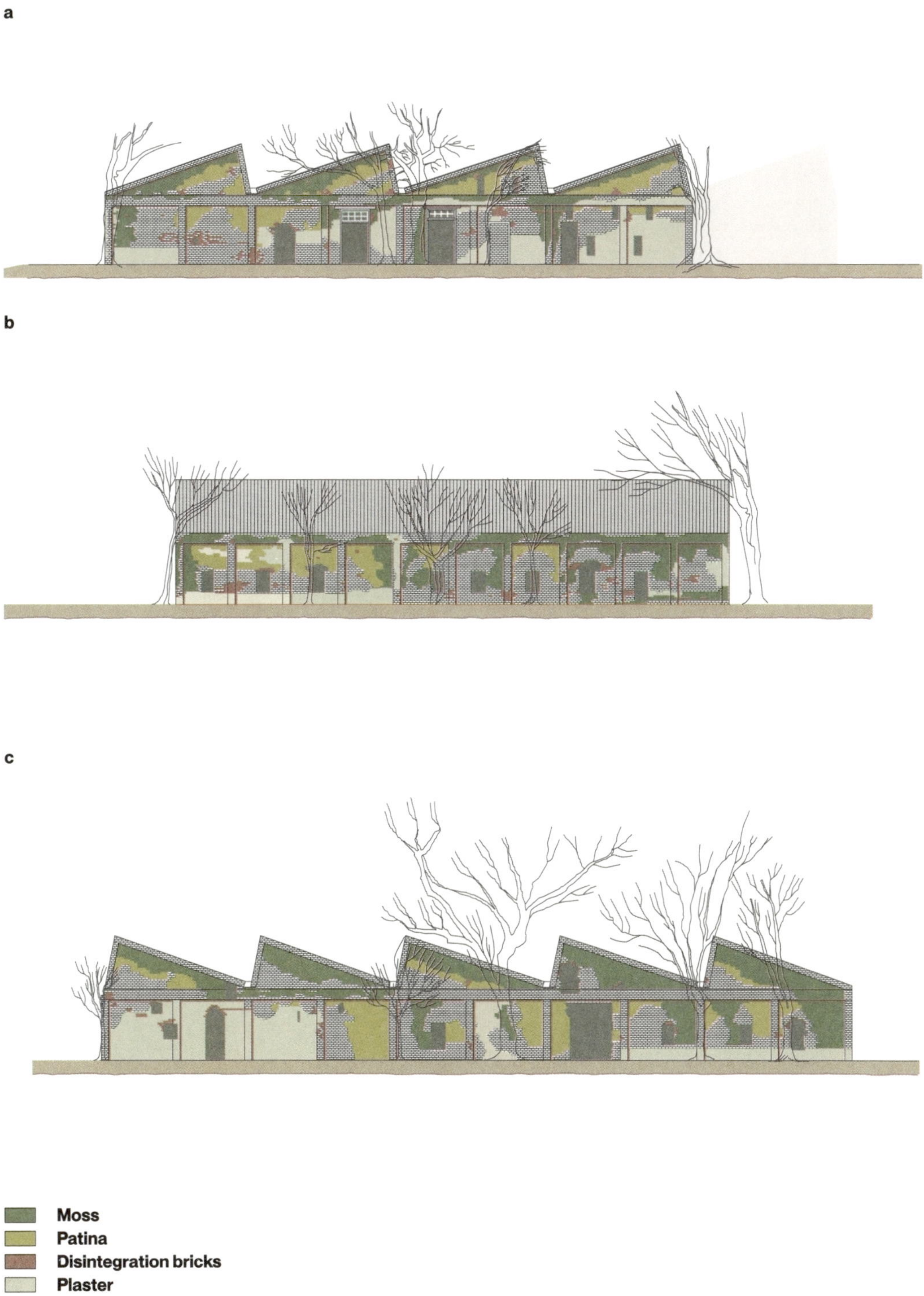

proximity of the neem (*Azadirachta indica*) and peepal (*Ficus religiosa*) trees. The entrapped water creates the ideal conditions for moss growth. As seen in the drawing, the protruding eaves and beams offer a shaded surface that resists evaporation. Since the wall faces east, exposure to sunlight is limited to the morning time, which is also conducive to moss growth. On the sections of the wall surface that receive some amount of sunlight, the moss is a dry green layer. Such sections are marked in yellow in the drawing. The moss fills the cracks and crevices between the bricks, forming an even, tight surface. These surfaces are soft to the touch. The texture turns rough as the dry moss starts to chip off, exposing a yellow layer of patina below. At places marked in green and yellow, the surface is firmer. As the rest of the surface continues to disintegrate, the brick becomes sparser. Receiving the most amount of sunlight during the day, the lower parts of the wall have been able to retain the plastered surface. Since water seepage from above has not yet reached this surface, the vegetative growth hasn't spread to this part of the wall.

The south-facing wall is a series of ten bays divided by columns. **Fig 3.1b** Large amounts of wet moss growth are observed toward the top of the wall, above and below the support beam. Ample shade from the neem, peepal, and gunda (*Cordia dichotoma*) trees toward the right half of the wall creates an appropriate condition for moss growth. The protruding beam, porous material, and shade from the tree foliage facilitate water retention, providing favorable moisture for vegetative growth on the ruined surface. Harsh sunlight reaches the surface toward the top-left corner, hence the dry green moss has turned into a yellow patina from overdrying. This patina is rough in texture and chips off with slight friction. When these layers fall off, the cracks between the bricks that were filled by the moss's growth are exposed.

The southeast corner of the wall has heavy vegetative growth because there is little to no direct sunlight and a high moisture content. On the southwest corner, the moss has turned into a dry patina because of direct sunlight. These areas suggest that the walls' vegetative receptivity heavily depends on exposure to direct sunlight.

Similarly, the surfaces of the west- and north-facing walls were mapped. **Fig 3.1c** The westward wall shows moss concentration on its upper surface, similar to the other walls. Despite receiving direct sunlight, the south-facing wall is heavily shaded by tree foliage, making it favorable for moss growth. In contrast, the north-facing wall does not receive direct sunlight yet does not show much moss growth; as there are no trees on this side, atmospheric heat is uniformly present, discouraging water retention on the wall's surface. In these cases, the presence or absence of trees has a greater effect on moss growth than the directionality of the wall.

The growth of moss on the ruinous walls is an assemblage enabled by moisture and heat that combines with matter from the disintegrating surface of the bricks. According to an architect's bias for clean, disinfected surfaces that privilege longevity, matter from disintegrating brick surface is considered dirt; thus, the receptive wall is "dirty" owing to moisture and heat. However, it is that dirt that is a driver of growth, namely the moss. Dirt reveals interspecies relationships. Theorist Hélène Frichot, following the work of Mary Douglas, argues that dirt is evidence of the interconnections and patterning of a world (Frichot 2019, 36; Douglas 1966, vii). Countering the architect's yearning for cleanliness, Frichot calls for a "dirty theory" to make architecture "think about the ordinary gestures of care, repair, and maintenance that can form part of its mandate" (Frichot 2019, 6). "Matter located where it is judged not to belong" (Frichot 2019, 9) is precisely what has caused sentience on the wall.

The vegetal growth's constant transformation in terms of size and color makes the fate of the wall uncertain. Advocating for precarity, Anna Tsing argues that even though such indeterminacy is frightening, it also makes life possible (Tsing 2015, 20). Indeterminacy is the producer of living systems at the ruin. Survival here is always interdependent and hence it is also necessarily subject to the indeterminacy of transformations of the self and others. Tsing argues that interspecies collaborations lead to changes both within and across species (Tsing 2015, 29). As the vegetal growth transforms, so does the wall that supports it. Both the wall and the vegetation are in constant flux, aiming for stability and survival, respectively.

In forming an assemblage, the vegetal growth, disintegrating brick wall, and moisture coexist as self-organized *meshworks* (DeLanda 1997, 32), which constantly give rise to a hybrid formed by the flow of matter and energy through the system. Meshworks are formed when a set of heterogeneous elements are superpositioned. These interconnections require catalysts or intercalary elements (DeLanda 1997, 64). The moss once formed on the disintegrated wall will attract and retain more moisture, leading to densification and the formation of a patina, thus becoming its own intercalary element. In this process, the composition of the wall changes through the propagation of the patina. Another aspect of the meshwork is its stabilization—the patina and wall stabilize each other as the moss densifies, filling the crevices of the disintegrated wall and hardening as a patina on the surface of the wall.

Conducive Condition of Surface Irregularity

The irregularity of the wall surface allows foraging species such as arboreal rodents, reptiles, birds, and insects to create their habitat in the ruins. Squirrels require continuity of surface for movement. The protruding beam provides a horizontal ledge that gives the squirrels a continuous path. Column protrusions provide gaps and non-slippery rough surfaces favorable to vertical movement. The exposed brick and cement textures give grip for movement. Squirrels do not like to move vertically for long stretches; hence, they move horizontally through available voids to break up the vertical movement. The wall's disintegration—perhaps caused by human vandalism—has created many spaces that give squirrels the opportunity to break from continuous vertical movement.

The construction of shelter and the storage and retrieval of food, as well as the movement required for these two activities, determine the way in which the ruin offers squirrels a favorable habitat. These rodents require a space where it is possible to store food. Hence tree hollows, an empty animal burrow, or even the attic of a house are the squirrel's choice of habitat. The Indian palm squirrel constructs a drey in the cavity of a tree, which it keeps camouflaged with leaves. The squirrel stays in the drey until the temperature outside is warm enough to move about. A drey consists of a platform made from woven twigs and a base made from compacted leaves. Small twigs are woven together to give the base a spherical shape. The gaps are filled in with soft materials such as twigs, moss, leaves, shredded bark, and even paper. Squirrels tend to construct their dreys at a height of twenty feet near the main trunk of the tree where several small branches meet. Some squirrels have multiple dreys. These nests require constant maintenance—the leaves and twigs need to replenished. The construction and maintenance of dreys make up much of a squirrel's everyday movements. The NC Mill ruin is in a forest-like setting with diverse deciduous trees, which squirrels like. People living nearby put out water in broken clay pots for birds and squirrels, which fulfills a requirement of these squirrels' habitat—tree-filled areas near permanent sources of freshwater.

Peepal Tree
Ficus religiosa

Gunda Tree
Cordia dichotoma

Squirrels gather and hoard food. They don't store all their food in one place but hide it in various caches buried underground. Multiple caches ensure safety against invasion by other squirrels who might find one of the reserves. They also store food for a short period of time, such as half-eaten nuts in branches to come back and eat a few hours later. Most of the day is thus spent not just gathering and storing food (alongside maintaining the dreys), but also tracking down food that had been hidden already. Squir-

Figure 3.2 Map of trees growing around the NC Mill structure in Ahmedabad, India.

rels use sight, touch, smell, and hearing to perceive their environment. Their claws firmly grip trees to help them climb and the ankles on their hind legs rotate 180 degrees, helping them go down a tree. They use sight, touch, and smell to find food, and carry food such as nuts, seeds, acorns, and berries in their cheeks. Memory and olfactory senses are weak in squirrels and sometimes they don't find their own food reserve. However, they might stumble upon another squirrel's cache, which they would steal from without hesitation (Bales 2024).

Squirrel paths are mapped on the elevation, and a relationship between these paths and surface irregularities is observed. The position of trees **Fig 3.2** in relation to the wall plays an essential role in creating paths for the squirrels. A peepal tree **Fig 3.3** leans against the top of the wall, creating niches and voids inhabited by pigeons (*Columba livia*), Asian koels (*Eudynamys scolopaceus*), and black kites (*Milvus migrans*). The west-facing wall **Fig 3.4a** demonstrates limited interactions with squirrels and various birds. The wall is heavily shaded by two large neem trees, whose vegetation is denser in the northwest corner, making it difficult for the animals to interact with the wall there. Indian peafowls (*Pavo cristatus*) walk along the edge of the roof or perch atop the dilapidated wall, feeding on the leaves and fruit that has fallen from the trees. The protruding beam makes space for their movement. This side of the wall has large openings toward the top.

Finding and accessing food primarily determine the way the Indian peafowls inhabit the ruin. Peafowls are foragers that have a highly varied diet of both plant and animal matter. The spacious, overgrown lands around the ruin have become a feeding ground for the peafowls. They often bask in the sun in the morning and during hot afternoons they rest in shaded areas. Though most of their food is acquired at ground level, they also fly up to the roof of the ruin to roost and survey the whole area. Their good eyesight helps them find food at a distance. At night, they roost on neem and other large trees around the ruin to keep away from predators. Other birds such as pigeons, red-ringed parakeets (*Psittacula krameri*), and mynas (*Acridotheres tristis*) rest and forage here as well. Pigeons and red-ringed parakeets have successfully adapted to living in disturbed habitats, especially urban environments that provide them with ambient temperatures and food—while both primarily feed on seeds, the latter also eat insects, fruits, and nectar. With their beaks and feet, they act as seed dispersers and pollinators. Pigeons are most often seen in the daytime and seek cover at night and during the heat of the day. They flock while roosting, sunning, and feeding, and are aggressively protective of their nest. Red-ringed parakeets are a secondary cavity-nester species—that is, they build their nests in holes that were dug by other species. Thus, the ruins be-

Figure 3.3 Peepal tree growing near a wall of NC Mill supports squirrel movements and the habitats of the Asian koel and black kite.

Figure 3.4 Disintegrating brick walls allow for movement, nesting, and resting of various rodent, animal, and bird species on the east-facing (a), south-facing (b), and west-facing (c) facades of NC Mill in Ahmedabad, India.

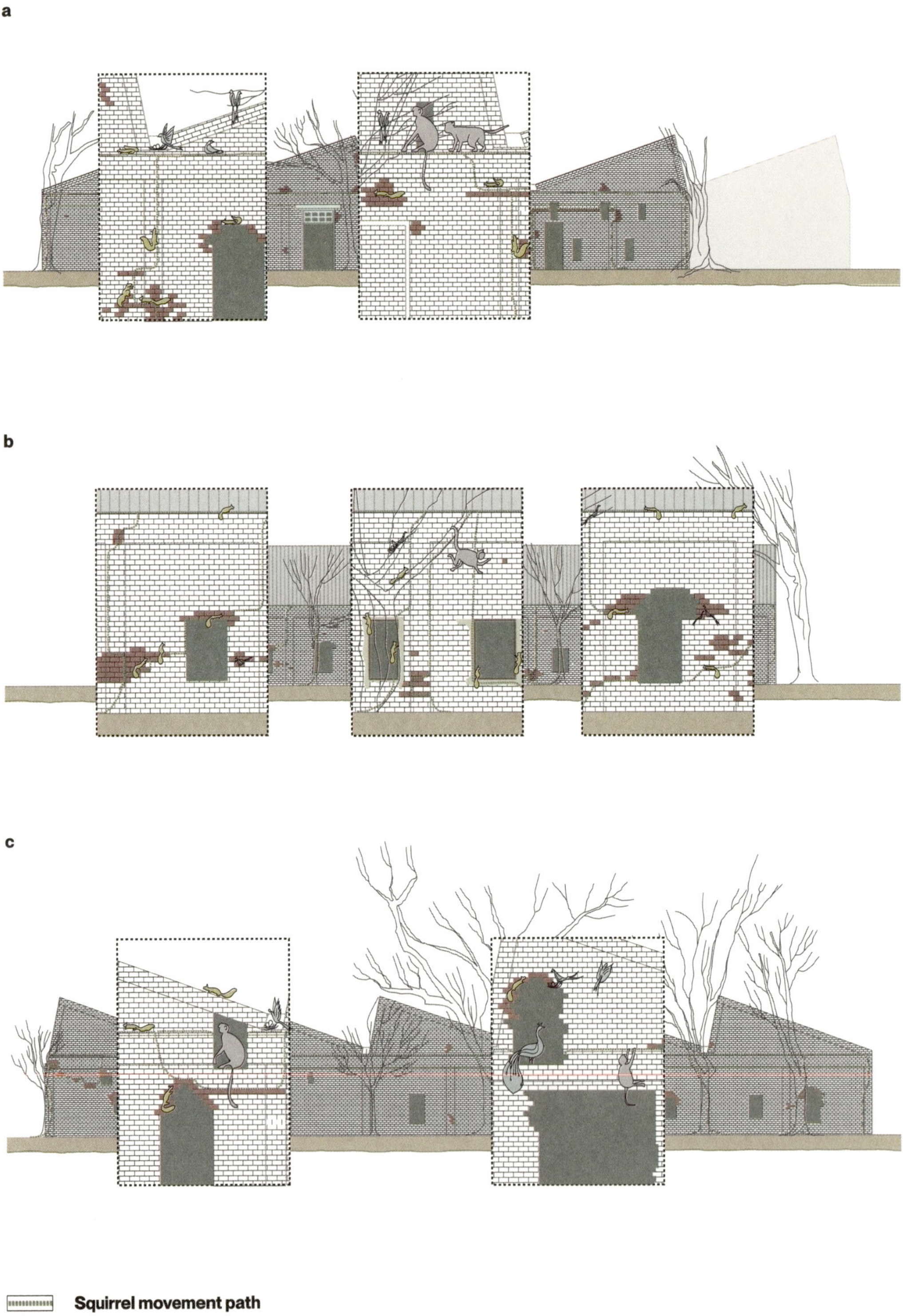

come a great opportunity for these species to find an already available cavity in which to nest. The red-ringed parakeet is motile, arboreal, and diurnal, and exhibits a torpor during every night (Flory 2019). This species is also sedentary and social, living in groups. It uses its vision to perceive the environment and acoustics to communicate. Squirrels are known to prey on the eggs of this bird.

The urban ruin is favorable to mynas, as they avoid dense vegetation, preferring the outskirts of a town and occupying homesteads in partly open forests. They aggressively defend their nests and forage in a territory averaging 117 square meters. This means that their existence is confined to the ruin. They communicate vocally with other mynas and their wide variety of alarm calls can warn other birds too. Their primary diet consists of fruit, grain, flower nectar, petals, grubs, and insects. However, they also prey on the eggs and young of other birds. The ruin also offers them small mammals such as mice, lizards, and small snakes, and spiders and earthworms, apart from the trash and food waste dumped by humans. They pollinate and disperse seeds for many plants and trees. They also act as hosts for various parasites, such as nematodes, tapeworms, trematode flukes, arthropods, and bird mites.

The wide-canopied deciduous trees such as the neem and banyan that surround the NC Mill provide the ideal conditions for food and shelter for the Asian koel, a shy bird that is more often heard than seen. During the day, they eat fruits directly from trees. They also consume insects, caterpillars, eggs, and small vertebrates. They play an important role in the dispersal of tree seeds, quickly regurgitating large-seeded fruits near the parent tree while ingesting and depositing small-seeded fruits at greater distances from the parent tree, contributing to the evolution of tree populations.

The large openings in the mill's walls caused by dilapidation are used by gray langurs (*Semnopithecus entellus*) to rest as they feed on the surrounding trees. These animals are diurnal and semi-arboreal, spending 80 percent of their time on the ground using quadrupedal locomotion. They use trees primarily for sleeping (Semke 2011). They use visual, tactile, acoustic modes for communication, and visual, tactile, acoustic, and chemical (taste and smell) modes for perception. They feed on leaves, fruits, flowers, insects, and other foods such as bark, gum, and soil. They prefer more developed leaves over young leaves. They are not highly selective foragers and consume human food when available. They remove fruit casings, which small bugs such as soapberry bugs (*Leptocoris augur*) eat. They also assist in dispersing seeds. They sleep in the upper-forest canopy to avoid predators. The ruin provides trees to safely roost in.

The south-facing wall, **Fig 3.4b** north-facing wall, **Fig 3.4c** and east-facing wall, all load bearing, are three-and-a-half bricks thick and demonstrate nine conditions of surface irregularities favorable to squirrels and birds. First, voids one to two bricks deep beneath the protuding beam provide space for nesting (building and inhabiting a nest) and roosting (perching to rest or sleep) for birds such as pigeons, Asian koels, and mynas. Second, surface irregularities—larger voids two to three bricks deep and three to four bricks wide—break the vertical continuity of squirrels' paths as they move along the wall's surface. Third, the depressed timber window frame provides a sheltered ledge-like surface for squirrels and lizards to rest on as well as move across. The edge of the frame acts as a guide for the route. Fourth, the protruding beam provides a horizontal pathway for squirrels and peafowls. Fifth, pieces of timber jutting out of the wall near the beam become surfaces for squirrels and birds to rest on. Sixth, moss-laden surfaces provide friction for squirrels as they move up and down the wall. Seventh, the horizontal spaces where bricks were removed make squirrels take a serpentine route as they move up the wall. Eighth, exposed cement surfaces near the windowsill and lintel provide friction for vertical movement. Ninth, larger openings above the beams on the west-facing wall are used by gray langurs to rest as they feed on the fruit of the surrounding trees.

Mapping reveals interactions between birds (pigeons, parakeets, mynas, koels, peafowls), rodents such as squirrels, and trees (growing in close vicinity to the ruin) necessitated partially because of disintegrating wall surfaces. Trees, birds, rodents, and bricks are in a continuous making and unmaking of one another. These interactions occur in a terrapolis, which Donna Haraway defines as a space offering opportunities to earthly beings for multispecies relationships (2016, 11). Haraway argues that the way to combat the current species loss is by partially recovering and creating spaces for cohabitation by working together. A liminal space or a threshold between human and nonhuman territories comprises the characteristics of both worlds and considers the needs of interspecies relations. It is a space for multispecies becoming-with.

Traditionally, architectural design has concentrated its energies providing function-specific spaces, making architecture deterministic. It has restricted itself to the binary of nature versus culture, where indoors is protected human territory and outdoors is the natural world. The terrapolis, on the contrary, is a space of and for indeterminacy. The ruin points us to the need to pay attention to thresholds, in-between spaces, spaces where multiple lifeworlds can overlap. It urges architects to think about creating conditions for life-forms to thrive, move, and find food, rather than determining absolute solutions for highly sterilized living environments.

Not all environmental assemblages are known to us. When conditions are created for multiple species to move and communicate, it is still impossible to predict the manner, intensity, magnitude, directions, and locations of multispecies interactions that will take place. This indeterminacy is precisely what makes the ruin a place of learning. Our reading of the ruin reveals that human-disturbed landscapes are ideal spaces for learning the histories humans have made in these places *and* the ongoing histories of nonhuman participants.

The surface irregularity of the decaying walls and the unused structural members behave as a prosthesis of the ruin. At the amputated, distressed, and fragile site, prosthetics help recover life. Vegetation grows over disused building elements and walls. Something redundant becomes a support for life. It is irrelevant to the purpose of the original but is made relevant by other life-forms that use it for support; later it becomes integral to these life-forms. Haraway calls it a hybrid, mosaic, chimera, cyborg—invoking prosthetics—where bodies do not end at their skin but go beyond it. In architectural thinking, introducing a prosthesis is key, something that is accessible, available, and usable.

Conducive Conditions of Dirt

The NC Mill is receptive to more-than-human species through the various materials available on-site, a large amount of which, considered *dirt* by humans, participate in collaborative interspecies survival. Three types of dirt are observed: fallen leaves from trees, the growth of scrub vegetation, and debris from the decaying structure. Traditionally, what is seen as dirt is cleaned out at the onset of an architectural project. Mapping this dirt reveals its capacity to host many species. The neem tree, peepal tree, gunda tree, bay leaf tree (*Laurus nobilis*), mahanimb tree (*Ailanthus excelsa*), banyan tree (*Ficus benghalensis*), and sandpaper tree (*Ehretia anacua*) shed dry leaves, creating a thick layer of organic matter on the ground around the mill. On a longer timescale, this layer receives water via precipitation and decomposes to create humus and enrich the soil. On a shorter timescale, the moisture trapped in the layer is receptive to worms, insects, and spiders, and the understory becomes a feeding ground for bird species such as the Indian myna, grey francolin (*Ortygornis pondicerianus*), and Indian peafowl. An anthropogenic perspective regards the layer of dried leaves as dirt and would get rid of it to achieve a clean surface, in the process losing a thick layer of decomposing, soil-enriching matter that hosts a complex ecosystem. Beneath the fallen leaves is the scrub vegetation growth of aakdo (*Calotropis procera*) and chanibor (*Ziziphus nummularia*). **Fig 3.5** These areas are highly receptive to many bird species: common tailorbirds (*Orthotomus sutorius*) flit among these scrubs, and Asian koel and Indian myna forage on these grounds, as the tall dry grass protects them against predators. Squirrels run and forage for food here too. Deemed as unwanted wild growth, such vegetation is cleared from urbanizing areas. This poses a great threat to the many birds, animals, and rodents that use the wild vegetation to find food and as protection from predators. The debris of broken bricks and concrete holds water from rain or dew, creating moist conditions for insects to nest in—for instance, ants use them as bases to build ant hills. The debris thus becomes a feeding ground for numerous birds and rodents. The debris, leaf litter, and dry-grass growth demonstrate how dirt is receptive to other species and creates conditions conducive to their growth.

Figure 3.5 Layers of dried leaves around the peepal tree growing in front of NC Mill's south facade.

Interdependencies at Pickers Mill

At Pickers Mill, we are greeted with hostile eyes and apprehensive looks. A person holding a puppy close to his face comes up and joins the crowd that has assembled, curious about the purpose of our visit. They resemble the image on the cover of Donna Haraway's 1991 book *Simians, Cyborgs, and Women: The Reinvention of Nature*, a painting by Lynn M. Randolph titled *Cyborg* (1989).

We move through the precinct both guided and followed by the crowd; it is as if the crowd surrounds us as we walk. The first room is locked, but through broken windows we see a pile of decaying leather pickers. In the next room there is a dead animal on which sunlight falls through a void in the fallen-in roof. Playing cards, plastic teacups, and empty bottles of alcohol are strewn among broken bricks. A gray langur sits in an opening created by the removal of bricks from a wall, holding a dead tree stump in one hand and a partially eaten cookie in the other. **Fig 3.6** This cookie is as industrial as an item of food can get. This image also conjures up Haraway's cyborg. The factory structure is fractured but seems held together by the trees that have clasped it with their roots, invading it, and yet ensuring that it stays.

The site is privately owned with plans to be converted into real estate and at the same time it is the location of seemingly adverse activities that ensure the workers' rights to the place and keep the property sharks away. The materiality of the ruin embodies those intimations of ambiguity and hostility in its broken walls, falling ceilings, strewn cards, dead animals, vegetation, and trees taken root in the walls, glassless north-facing skylights against corroded trusses. It hosts a visibility to the outside and yet a lingering invisible antagonism that comes from lack of accessibility. The dichotomy between socially acceptable uses of space and antisocial activities has traditionally been the basis of what Haraway calls the "border war [comprising] the territories of production, reproduction, and imagination" (Haraway 2016a, 7). Instead, the coexistence can be reunderstood as a cyborg—one that has no "origin story" (Haraway, 2016a, 43), one that reassembles itself.

Mapping Sentience undertakes a close examination of the ruination process of the precinct—seen in the ways human vandalism coincides with vegetation that has taken shelter in the building such that the former renders the structure vulnerable and the latter makes it stronger. The ecology of the ruinous site—manifested in vegetation growing out of broken walls, or corroding steel, or people finding ways to survive—demands a redefinition of revitalization that incorporates a sentience into the otherwise derelict place. Haraway's rejection of binaries supports a multiplicity of meanings that emerge because the ruins and waste—redundancy and uselessness—escape the confines of norms surrounding their previous value or function. In this liberation, designers, preservationists, and users alike can relate to these mean-

Figure 3.6 Gray langur eating a ParleG biscuit at the Pickers Mill ruin in Ahmedabad, India.

ings in "imaginative, sensual, conjectural and playful fashion [because it is...] precisely their fragmentary nature and lack of fixed meaning that renders industrial ruins more profoundly meaningful" (Edensor 2005, 123). When abandoned mills in Ahmedabad are sited on a city plan, their urban relational network starts to appear related to issues such as land value and livability. The Pickers Mill was once linked to other mills in the vicinity, which depended on it for a regular supply of pickers. The collapse of one mill affects other mills. The Pickers Mill was the epicenter of a neighborhood of factory workers who needed access to public facilities such as schools, shops, parks, and libraries. A quick survey reveals that these amenities are located within a one-kilometer radius from the mill but are no longer accessible to the factory workers. The mill site as a ruin is detached from the urban milieu and has turned itself inward. It is now an emerging ecosystem, combining a palette of decaying building materials and elements, changing spatial configurations, dumped trash, forgotten industrial machine parts, vegetation, and animal life. The ruin is receptive. It provides space and opportunity for vegetation to seed, take shape, sustain, thrive, and invade. In turn, it invites animals and birds to become part of the ruin. Mapping Sentience at the Pickers Mill is to map its receptivity. In its vandalized state, it becomes more receptive, offering new opportunities for the movement of animals and plants, heightening a state of collective aliveness.

Receptivity of the Ruin

The Pickers Mill is strewn with plastic items **Fig 3.7**. It is constantly being subjected to dilapidation, and signs of damage appear as debris piles up. Figure 3.8 maps the presence of mixed organic and plastic waste on site as well as building debris such as dirt. Similarly, stagnant water that collects during the rainy season is mapped to identify the productive possibilities of such dead and decaying matter. Mapping the presence of dirt, stagnant water, and debris shows how topographic changes to the site could be made.

Figure 3.9 maps animal (and human) interactions with the trees in the Pickers Mill precinct. The central banyan tree can be heard before it is seen, because its fruit attracts bird species such as parrots, koels, and mynas and other animals. Similarly, the long-stalked leaves of the peepal and sacred fig trees clatter noisily in the slightest breeze. The ripe figs attract fruit-eating bats and several birds such as the coppersmith, common mynah, golden oriole, Asian koel, red-ringed parakeet, and red-vented bulbul, who depend on the tree for their diet. Monkeys rarely spare the fruits of the jamun tree (*Syzygium cumini*), and many humans pick these treats as well. The jamun is a tall tree with a thick trunk, bearing fruit after eight years of its planting. The jamun fruit is green when young, and during the summer it becomes purple when it ripens, finally falling to the ground and creating a purple bed on the floor. The jamun flowers form an important part of the honeybee's diet. Goras ambli (*Pithecellobium dulce*), also known as foreign tamarind or jungle jalebi, is also present at the urban ruin. The tree reaches a height of about ten to fifteen meters and is drought resistant, which allows it to thrive in the arid conditions of urban Ahmedabad. It has a spiny truck, bipinnate leaves, and greenish-white, fragrant, sessile flowers that produce a pod that turns pink when ripe and opens to expose the seed arils, a pink or white sweet-and-sour edible pulp relished by various animals. Cows and goats can also feed on its leaves. The pulp contains

Figure 3.7 Playing cards disposed among the debris at the Pickers Mill in Ahmedabad, India.

Figure 3.8 Map of Pickers Mill showing the presence of debris, organic waste, and water in the ruin precinct.

black shiny seeds that are circular and flat. Birds that feed on the pulp help to disperse the seeds. The Goras ambli is a host for the common nawab (*Polyura athamas*), three-spot grass yellow (*Eurema blanda*), and bright babul blue (*Azanus ubaldus*) caterpillars, and several moths, contributing to pollination. Ruminants and rabbits occasionally use neem leaves as forage.

The interaction of vegetation with the structure of the mill appears in three systems Fig 3.10. The aerial roots of the banyan tree snuggle against the walls, getting closer and more violent as

Figure 3.9 Map of trees growing around the Pickers Mill structure and various bird species found among them, 2018.

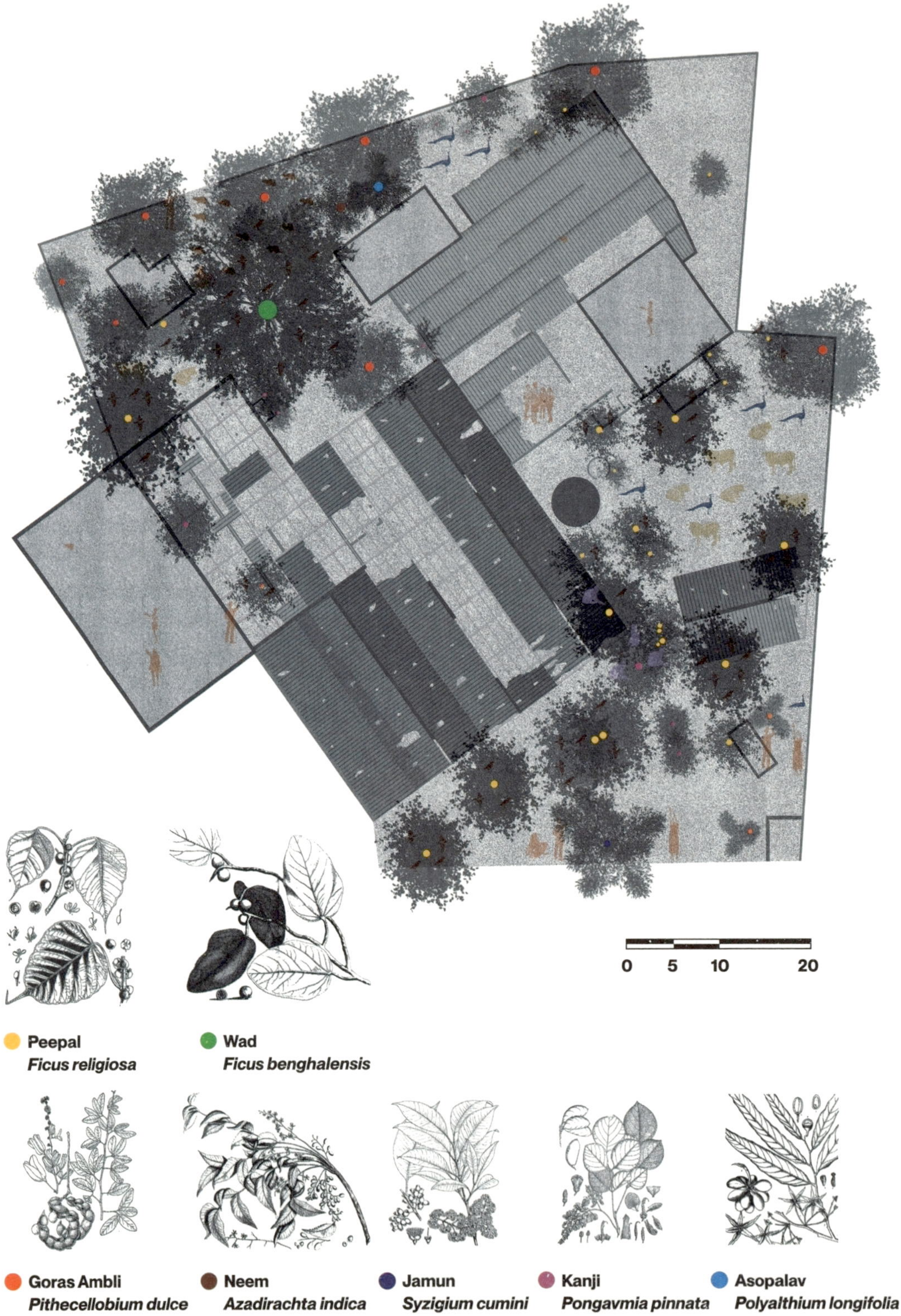

they penetrate and finally strangle the structure, disintegrating certain parts but also stabilizing others in a composite structure of tree, brick, and concrete. The banyan is a fig that starts its life as an epiphyte (a plant that grows on another plant) when its seed germinates in a crack or crevice of a host tree or edifice. The seeds are small and because most banyans grow in woodlands, a seedling that germinates on the ground is unlikely to survive. However, many seeds fall on the branches and stems of other trees or on human structures, and when they germinate they grow roots toward the ground and consequently may envelop part of the host tree or edifice. The roots of the peepal tree can act similarly, also leading to the destruction and stabilization of something new. The neem tree, on the other hand, likes to stay away from the structure. It prefers to have its own space. Trunks of peepal and kanji trees (*Pongamia pinnata*) merge with the base of the wall and lean onto the wall as if in an embrace in places. The foliage interacts with the roof by creating a canopy, forming a detached cover, or completely replacing the roof. The banyan, peepal, neem, and jamun foliage—in their adjacency to the structure—form a canopy sheltering the open space to make an extended space that emerges from the abandoned structure. The kanji, banyan, neem, and peepal foliage form a cover over the galvanized iron-sheeted truss, in some places completely replacing the glass panes that used to be there. The kanji tree is self-seeding and its lateral roots grow up to nine meters in two decades. Its pink and lilac flowers blossom throughout the year, forming a fragrant ornamental canopy over the ruin. The neem is a drought-resistant, fast-growing deciduous tree that reaches a height of fifteen to twenty meters. Its branches are wide and sprawling, with a dense round foliage from twenty to twenty-five meters in diameter.

In the examples above the structure of the abandoned mill demonstrates its capacity to receive the elementals such as tree roots, birds, and animals. Here, human activity does not frame the elementals. Instead, its leftover evidence in the form of ruin starts to embrace them. With a phenomenological approach, Amanda Boetzkes follows the earth art movement of the late 1960s to show that art can play a role in critiquing the ways we frame nature by forging an aesthetic awareness of how nature exceeds its discourses and representation. More than using land as a sculpting medium, earth art interrogated how the overwhelming presence of nature problematizes the drive to represent. Boetzkes argues that the earth is not a site that can be subjected to human

Roots and Structure

Snuggle

Penetrate

Strangle

Trunk and Wall

Canopy and Roof

signification. Instead, it is only available to human senses in its materiality. It resists its representation (such as a drawing or a photograph), "overflowing" the field of human perception (Boetzkes 2010, 4). Earth artists create conditions of possibility for the earth to appear. Here, earth has the agency to reveal itself and is independent of human representation. In Boetzkes's articulation of the earth art movement, receptivity becomes a significant way of engaging with the elemental, which can be extrapolated to landscapes as sites of human intervention to derive methods of reading the ruin and subsequent architectural acts that let elementals exceed how humans represent them. The various life-forms of the ruin are elementals. Reading the ruin as receptive, we become aware of how it is constantly making space to accommodate new and growing life-forms. To be receptive is to have a vacancy. It is also to make space for an adjacent elemental to become comfortable. It is to displace oneself and to contain others. It is to receive rather than superpose. We see the deteriorated mortar of the mill's walls being displaced to accommodate tree roots that stabilize the weak walls. The wall, in its fragility, is receptive. The walls offering support to the neem and peepal trees, or the roof combining with the canopies of the adjacent trees, are similar examples of receptivity.

Drawing on the earth artists, architects can consider taking a similarly receptive stance while designing. This understanding opens up an opportunity to relocate the architect's position in relation to the elemental or the more-than-human. Archi-

Figure 3.10 Systems of interactions between trees and the mill structure at the Pickers Mill site.

tects may attempt to confront the site with designs that are withdrawn—that is, that aim for receptivity. To design receptive surfaces and spaces is to present the elementals and refrain from providing for them; instead, acknowledging and working with the agency and specificity of each, undertaking restraint in design. The needs of the elementals are different from those of humans. To become aware of those needs, we need to stop projecting our own needs and sensibilities onto the elemental. To withdraw, to recede from the elemental, generates the elemental's exaggerated otherness. It thus exaggerates the elemental's unintelligibility and indeterminacy, giving it the agency to express its own needs. Such an approach in architecture lets the site trigger the elementals' response-ability—their ability to respond to their environment.

The ruin is a place where cyborgs take shape. A cyborg is a hybrid of machine and organism (Haraway 2016a, 5). The remnant metal armatures of the ruin's roof and the vandalized decaying walls are part of an erstwhile machine—a factory building. The trees that have taken over and consolidate the structure are living organisms. The eventual composite is a cyborg. It is "resolutely committed to partiality, irony, intimacy, and perversity" (Haraway 2016a, 9). The trees and the structure are intimate: they exist because of each other, and hence coexist. Nature (tree) and culture (mill) are reworked; one can no longer be a resource appropriated or incorporated by the other. The relationships of hierarchical domination are challenged in these cyborgian shapes (Haraway 2016a, 9).

Conducive Conditions of Vandalism

Tall basins that were used in the leather tanning process stand prominently in the center of Pickers Mill. Today, they are used as seats by the people from the neighborhood in new spatial configurations. The structure's brick walls are now punctured with several holes of varying shapes and sizes. These holes—signifiers of human vandalism—are potentials for new spatial connections. They offer two types of readings: first, providing the visitor physical access through destroyed walls, and second, providing visual connection through which one can see and move—an enfilade. The map shows vandalism of the wall. **Fig 3.11** Some holes are high enough for a human to pass through (a, e). The second hole is large, starts four feet above the floor, and has ledges (d), which allow people to pass through as well as sit on it. A hole in the roof of one of the rooms visual access between the floors (f). A hole at human eye level allows for a conversation from one room to another (c). In places, one layer of brick has been removed to form an alcove-like space (g). Small holes above the lintel appear almost as peepholes (b). Bricks have been removed along the entire height of the wall in one instance (h).

Figure 3.11 Diverse punctures on the surface of Pickers Mill in Ahmedabad, India.

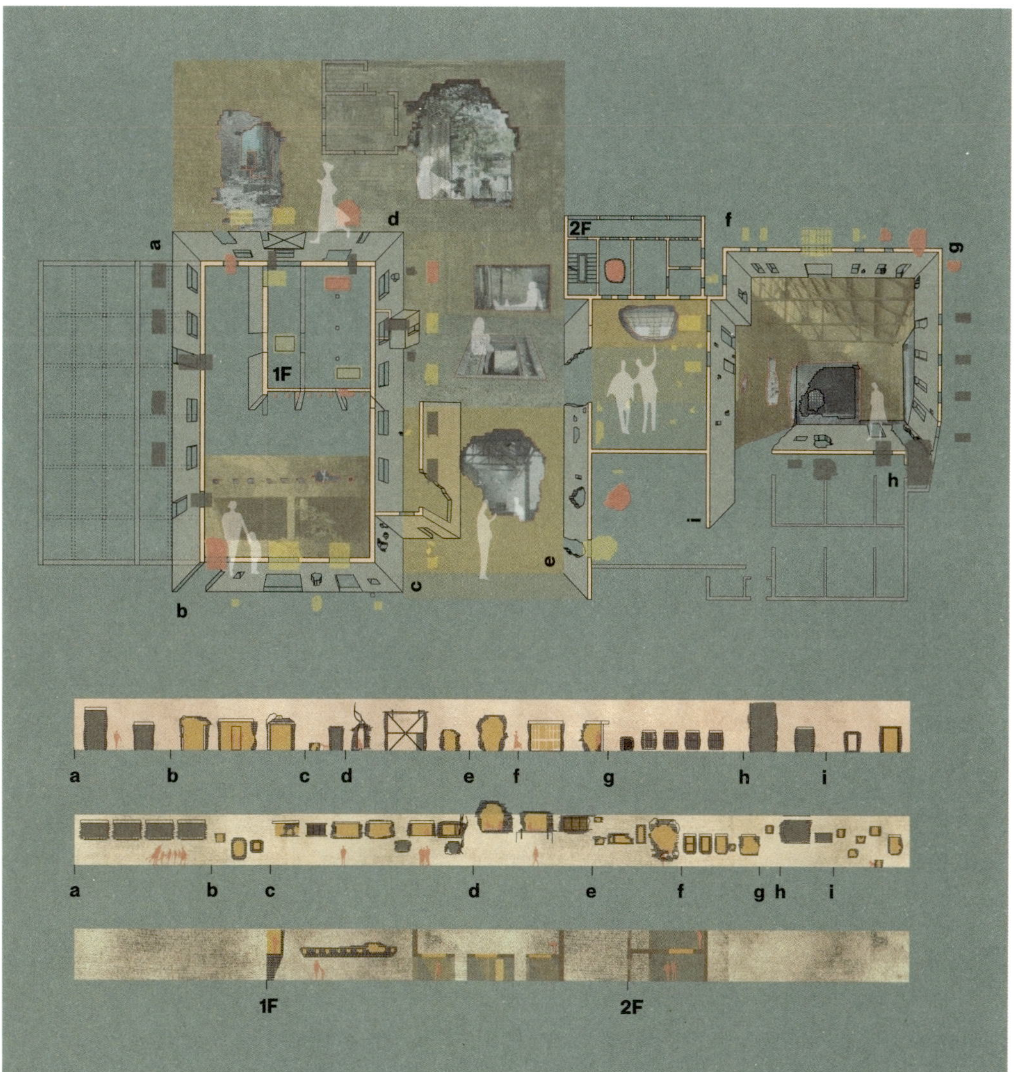

Vandalism is destroying something created by humans. In discourses such as architecture that tend toward sterile beauty and aesthetics, vandalism carries a negative connotation, since it is seen as a contamination of the original built form. However, contamination is not all bad, as Tsing has argued. “We are contaminated by our encounters, they change who we are as we make way for others,” she observes (Tsing 2015, 27). Contamination is necessary because it initiates new ways of inhabiting the ruin, new spatial relationships, new accesses, and new proximities. In this way of reading the ruin, architects are asked to revisit the discipline’s necessity for maintaining the status quo of the building, especially historical or heritage structures. Similar to Tsing’s argument that human disturbance sustains ecology (Tsing 2015, 160), vandalism opens the assemblage for transformative encounters, making new assemblages possible.

Interdependencies at an Abandoned Basalt Quarry in Champaner

Mapping Sentience acknowledges the abandoned quarry as a space that presents a tactile and layered spatiality (Mithal 2021, 147). Tactility here manifests in the geological composition of the site, mostly basalt combined with rhyolite, sandstone, loose soil, and clay deposits, and in the organic composition, mainly decaying plant matter, algal growth, dead animal remains, and new and surviving vegetation. The site assembles itself in the form of a ruin that persists primarily because it is constantly renewed through multispecies activity. The layered spatiality reveals itself in the way the site is fragile, disintegrating as well as consolidating. By recognizing the absence of a binding force that would hold pieces of a broken rock together, we acknowledge the fragility manifested in the fractured rocks. By recognizing those geological forces that cause sedimentation, we acknowledge the stabilities manifested in the amalgamating basalts and rhyolites. Disintegration and consolidation occur because material forces have taken certain orientations. Water travels along certain routes on the cliff face and on the ground, gets trapped in crevices along the way, slows down when it encounters a weed somewhere, gets burdened with clay somewhere else, and slows down further. Its speed, directionality, and intentionality, combined with the fractured condition of the quarry, give rise to new habitat conditions for various life-forms. Weight, gravity, and topography contribute to making the quarry a site for multispecies habitation.

The process of mapping and identifying disintegration and fragility begins with the navigation of the site. Navigation of a post-anthropocentric landscape is a deeply intense, material experience that emphasizes the shared character of earthly beings. Similar to embodied navigation at the mills, humans here avoid discomfort as an evolutionary defense mechanism against harm. As a result, we are tempted to walk the site through familiar cues, moving along desire paths formed over time through a history of movement—of humans, animals, water runoff, and vegetation Fig 3.12. Desire paths are a method of recording. Here, the movement of humans and animals is imprinted on the land, as the landscape records these movements as testimony to its history. The navigating body finds comfort in the familiarity and security of these imprints, which testify that these paths have been taken previously by others. We encounter unfamiliarity in inaccessibility caused by dense vegetation, steep terrain, or a fragile cliff

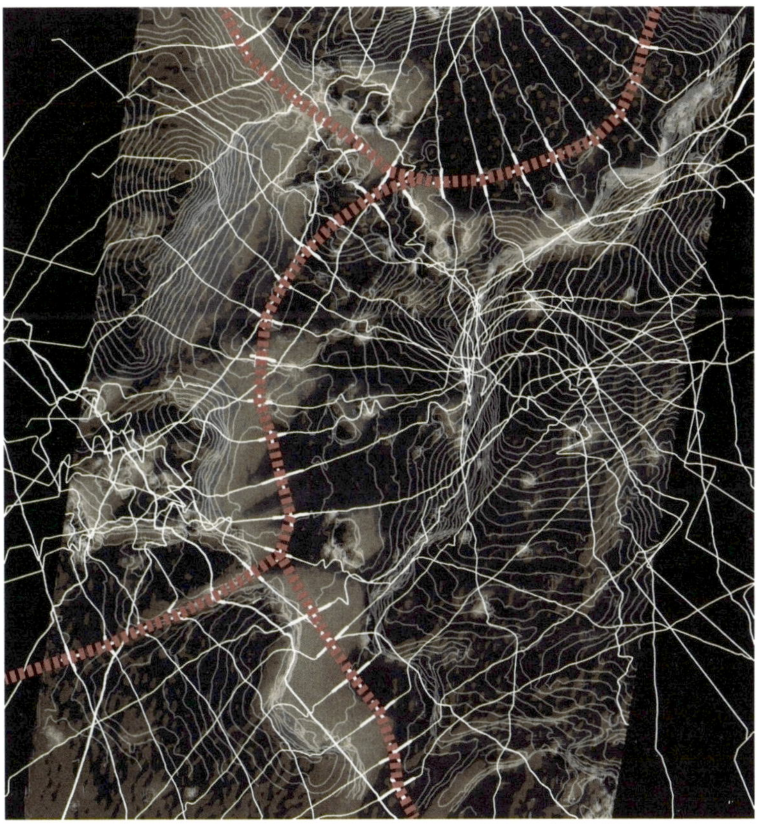

Figure 3.12 Materiality mapped while walking in the abandoned basalt quarry in Champaner, India.

with falling rocks. We encounter intimidating objects such as a shed snakeskin, a porcupine quill, and skeletal remains of cattle—intimidating because they suggest a certain deadness, a decay. They also suggest renewal. These encounters heighten our awareness, making us cautious as we approach, tread, and move through the place.

The blasted cliff face is a fractured face, broken into horizontal cracks. It appears as an agglomerate of densely packed basalt columns. Grass grows in horizontal layers where it finds ledge-like surfaces on the rock face that can retain soil and moisture. Algae and lichen grow in a vertical manner—tracing the routes and locations where rainwater streams down the cliff—an environment conducive to their growth. The roots of the vegetation invade the cracks and crevices on the cliff face. This rock surface is more consolidated and stronger than the areas where rocks are easily removed by touch, which do not have any binding force to hold them, either exerted by adjacent rocks or offered by forms of biological colonization. Fissures and fractures across the hillside provide unique opportunities for organic and inorganic materialities owing to the property of the vacancies. Each vacancy has unique visual and tactile properties forging unique coalitions with other proximate terrestrial, geological, vegetal, and animal presences. Bees hive and proliferate in niches in the cliff face that provide shade throughout the day and regulate temperature without obstructing passage or ventilation. Linear pathways and ledges provide an even surface and a directionality for cattle movement. We circumvent the water pool at the bottom of the quarry, its edges lined with basalt boulders. Atop a rock that touches the land and water is a recently shed snakeskin. We throw a stone tied to a rope into the water. It goes down almost five meters. That act concludes our embodied navigation of the site and commences our course of Mapping Sentience.

Mapping Sentience begins with recognizing familiarities, such as the desire paths that enable us to access and observe the site comfortably and safely. But by acknowledging the discomforting and hostile elements, we observe unique emergent multispecies interdependencies and interactions that are either symbiotic or parasitic in nature. Mapping Sentience in relation to disintegration also involves recognizing the interdependencies that are self-organized phenomenologically because of the accidental and available proximities of various actors—their origins, directions taken, alignments offered, and familiarities forged. For example, a rock that might fall off or destabilize a consolidated cliff owing to external forces might be hostile for humans but create unique opportunities for nonhuman actors to thrive.

At the abandoned quarry, Mapping Sentience charts waste, abandonment, and the materiality of redundancy. It identifies the ways in which the site rejuvenates itself by identifying where conditions of ruination and fracture have adapted themselves to become conditions for renewal and stabilization. The mappings make a case for the ecotone as a framework for intervention that gives meaning to ruins, vacancy, and hybrid forms of coexistence among various animate and inanimate forms. Geospatial data and manual investigations have been used to visualize these mappings.

Sentience here, is first mapped through found evidence of hybridity to identify how seemingly incongruent materials—organic and inorganic—form a symbiotic existence; and second, through found vacancies formed by broken basalt to identify how space—in terms of surfaces and edges—gets created when stone breaks along a line of structural weakness. In mapping these conditions, the site begins to reveal itself as a self-organized system that uses the potential of decay and ruination to regenerate both itself and its context. Vegetal and animal species as well as hydrological and geological entities are treated as elementals with agency because of their physical, chemical, and biological characteristics. The site, then, is read as a system where elementals can exercise their agency to thrive, proliferate, invade, or sustain owing to the conducive conditions made available to them.

Figure 3.13 Rock types are observed at the abandoned basalt quarry in Champaner, India.

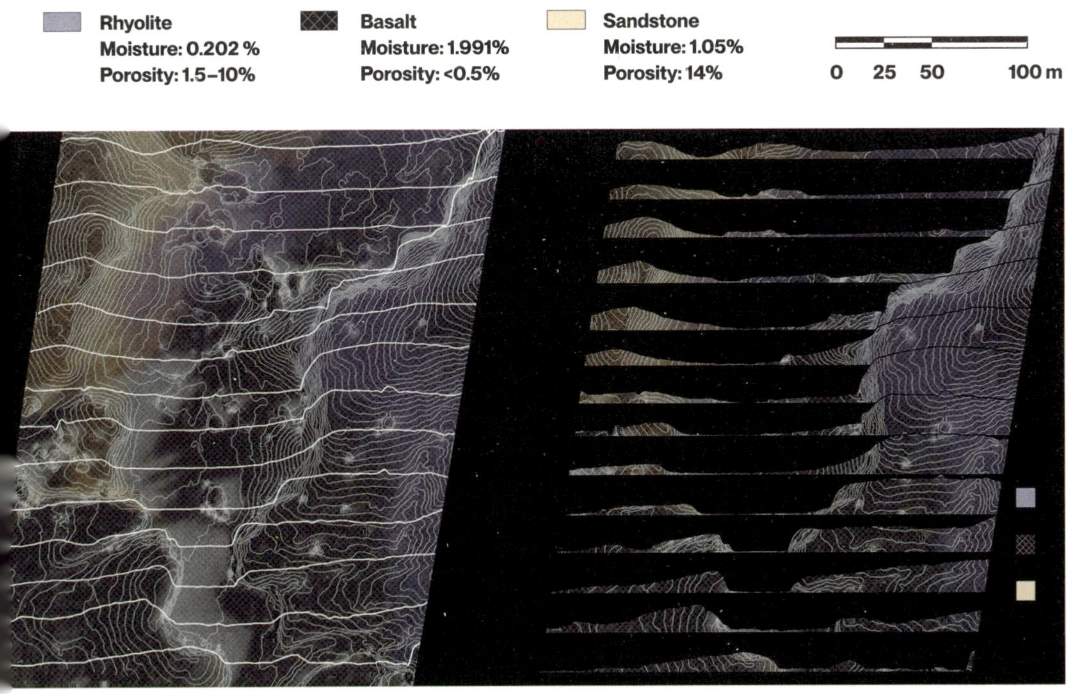

Conducive Condition of Disintegration and Eventual Hybridity

Three main rock types are observed at the quarry—basalt, rhyolite, and sandstone. The map in figure 3.13 spatializes the minerals, geological elements, and materials that form the quarry. Rhyolite occurs at lower elevations, ending in sandstone formations closer to the foothill. The rhyolite found here is red, pink, and purple, and also includes olivine (green), feldspar (white), biotite (black), hornblende (black), and quartz. The sandstone is yellow, orange, and brown, and also includes hornblende, biotite, quartz, and orthoclase. The basalt is black, gray, and green, and has the same additions as rhyolite. Most of the hill face is basalt. Figure 3.14 shows the combination of rhyolite and basalt observed on-site.

Figure 3.14 Rhyolite and basalt hybrid seen at the abandoned basalt quarry in Champaner, India.

The site is fragile because of disintegration due primarily to blasting and quarrying but also to continued weathering, erosion, and animal grazing at the top of the hill. Figure 3.15 shows the blasted rock as a series of drawings in the form of plans and sections with the location of fissures based on a visual survey. Blasting has scarred the hill face in the form of hexagonal fractures **Fig 3.16** that run along the surface and are not too deep, owing to the density of basalt. The second form of disintegration is due to the pieces of rock left behind after the blasting. These loose rocks, both big and small, are swept along with rapid water movement during monsoons or slip slightly when disturbed by wind or animal movement. Piles of debris formed during and in the aftermath of the blasting are in the process of consolidation, the lower layers being sedimented under the weight of the overlying stone deposit. The closer the disintegrated rocks are to the ground, the higher their chances of being consolidated. Mapping Sentience reads consolidation as a condition of renewal—offering stable surfaces for habitats for humans and nonhumans.

The continuous movement of humans and animals atop the quarry has created a path where plants no longer grow. Cattle grazing exposes the topsoil, making it more susceptible to the effects of wind and water erosion. The loose soil can be carried down with rainwater and wind, and accumulates in indentations in the rock surfaces, causing hybrids to form. **Fig 3.17** Some of these hybrids are described here.

Figure 3.16 Hexagonal fractures from the blasting of the rock at the abandoned basalt quarry in Champaner, India.

Figure 3.17 Hybrid formation between the rock vacancy, soil, and vegetation at the abandoned basalt quarry in Champaner, India.

When rainwater encounters the hexagonal ruptures of the fragile basalt rock, it adapts its movement to the available contingencies of directionality, elevation, and horizontality. Routes of surface runoff **Fig 3.18** indicate the location of water-caused weathering and erosion based on a fluid simulation in the topographical model and identify locations on the hill face where water can be observed seeping out. Moisture is retained in most of the routes. In turn, moving water carries loose rock and clay along with contributing to erosion. Since basalt is a dense rock and its cracks are not too deep, water deposits clay into these crevices. The hybrid here is of vacancy, stone, clay, and water **Fig 3.19**. As these crevices are rather shallow, sunshine reaches the moisture and clay, assisting plant growth. Sunlight causes the minerals and nutrients in the clay deposits to grow vegetation; in due time, the cracks become places of vegetation. The emergent hybrid of the stone's crevices and hard surface, water, nutrient-rich clay, and sunshine is an essential condition for a fragile landscape **Fig 3.20**. This mutates into a new hybrid when the vegetation grows, trying to stabilize itself by binding to the weakened rock **Fig 3.21**. Mapping Sentence reads this stabilization as a result of hybridity.

As trees grow, their roots find their way into the gaps of the rock face and grab onto the rock. The roots hold broken rock together, as well as consolidate the loose clay, forming a new hybrid of tree roots and stone. This hybrid also causes the weaker parts of the stone to fall away and accumulate at the base of the quarry, contributing to the cycle of sedimentation. Plant roots decompose when they die and release carbon dioxide, which, if converted to carbonic acid chemically, breaks down the rock into nutrient-rich soil that can absorb water. The hybrid here is of stone, roots, and soil.

Figure 3.15 Mapping disintegration and consolidation at the abandoned basalt quarry in Champaner.

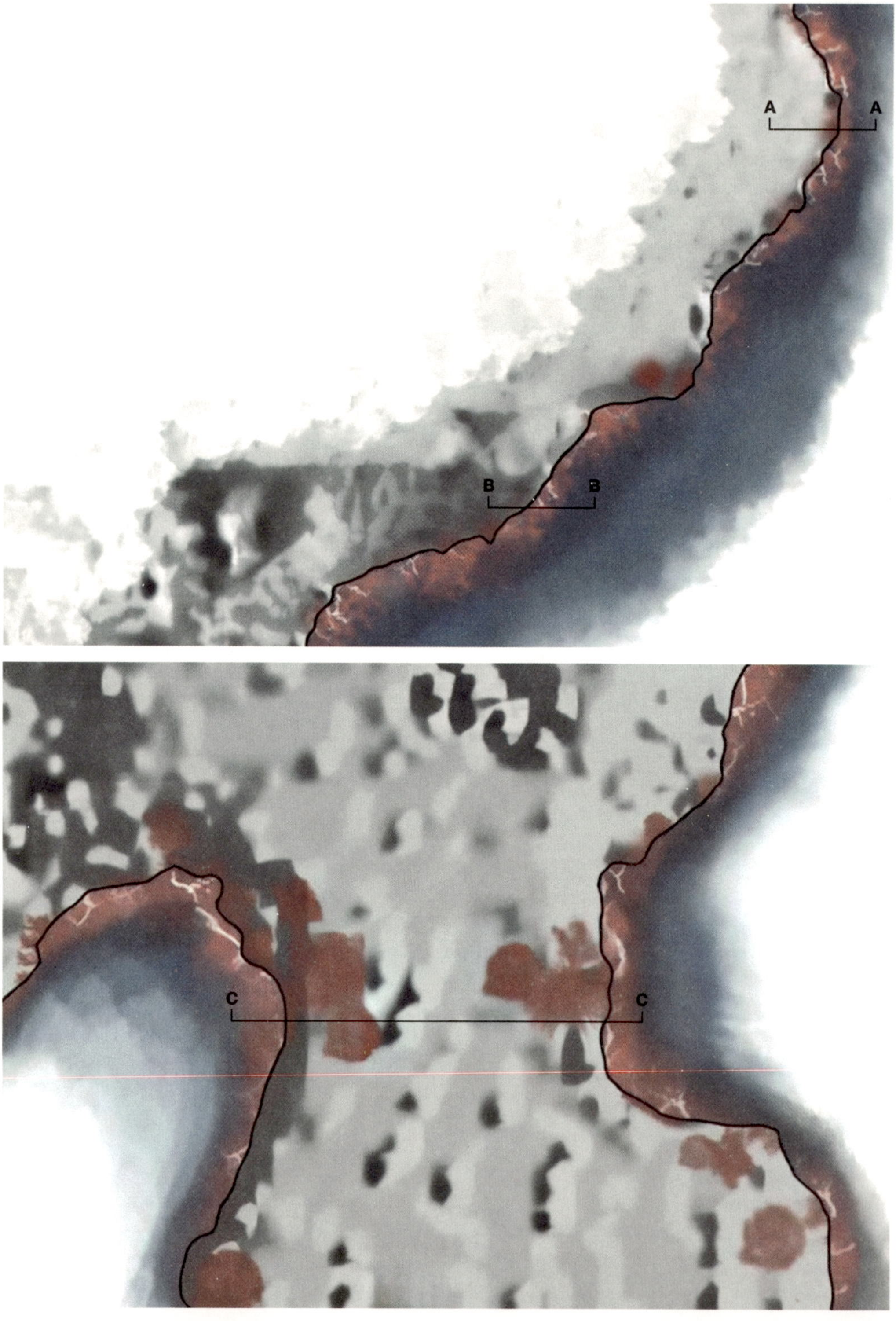

Cliff / Rock formation
Disintegration / Consolidation
Moisture
Vegetation

Section AA

Section BB

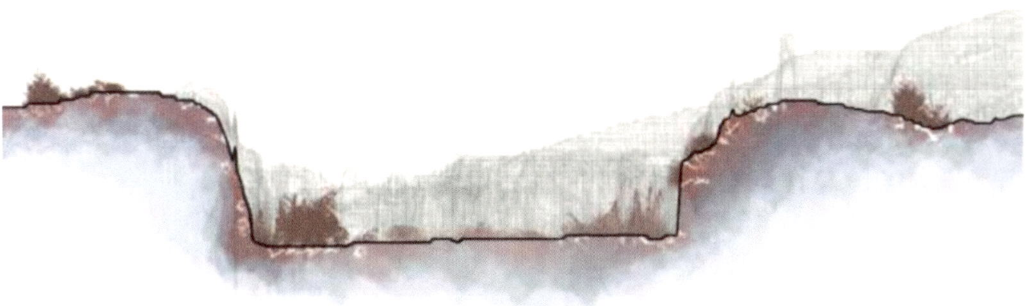

Section CC

Figure 3.18 Mapping water routes at the abandoned basalt quarry in Champaner, India.

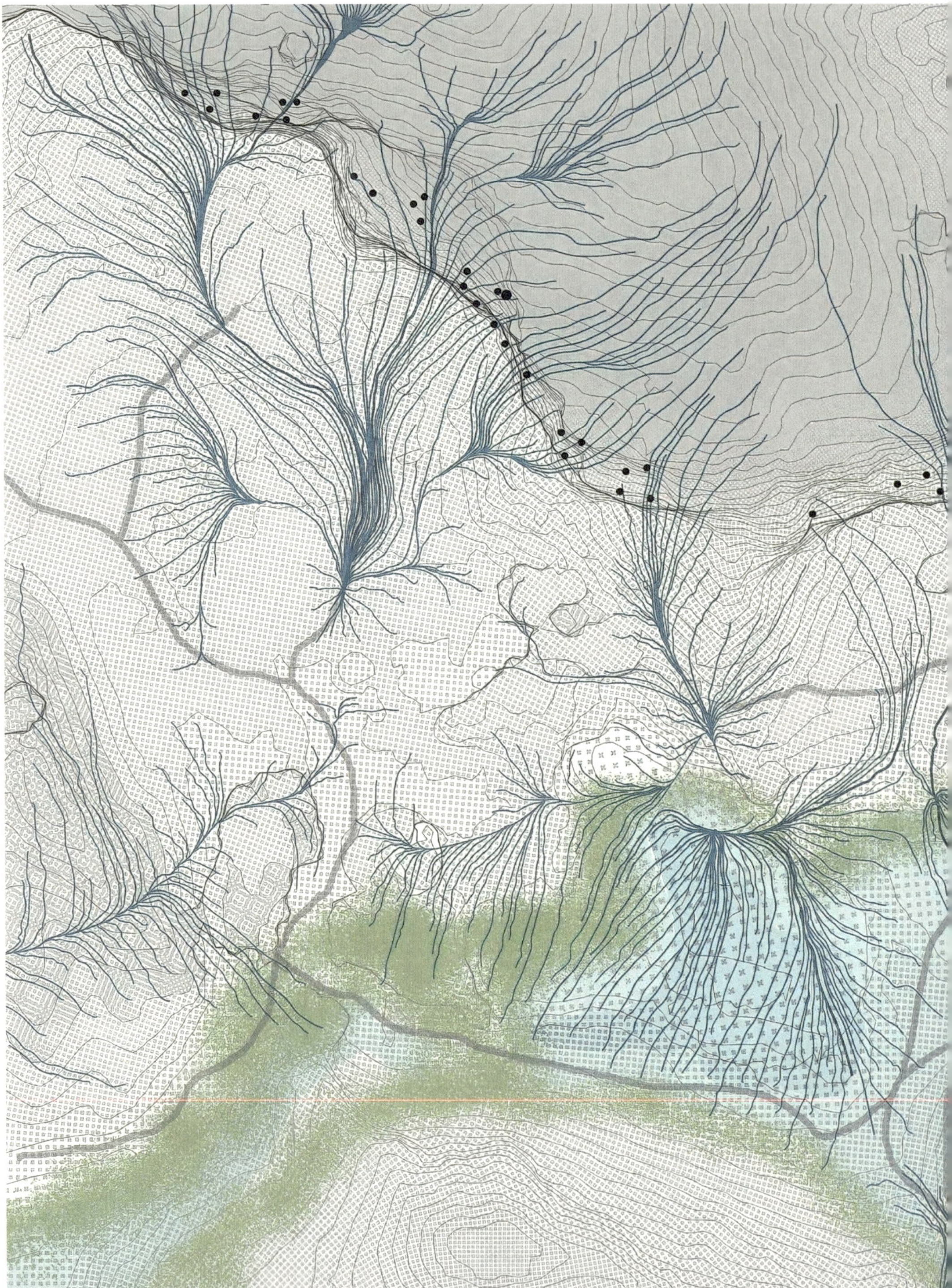

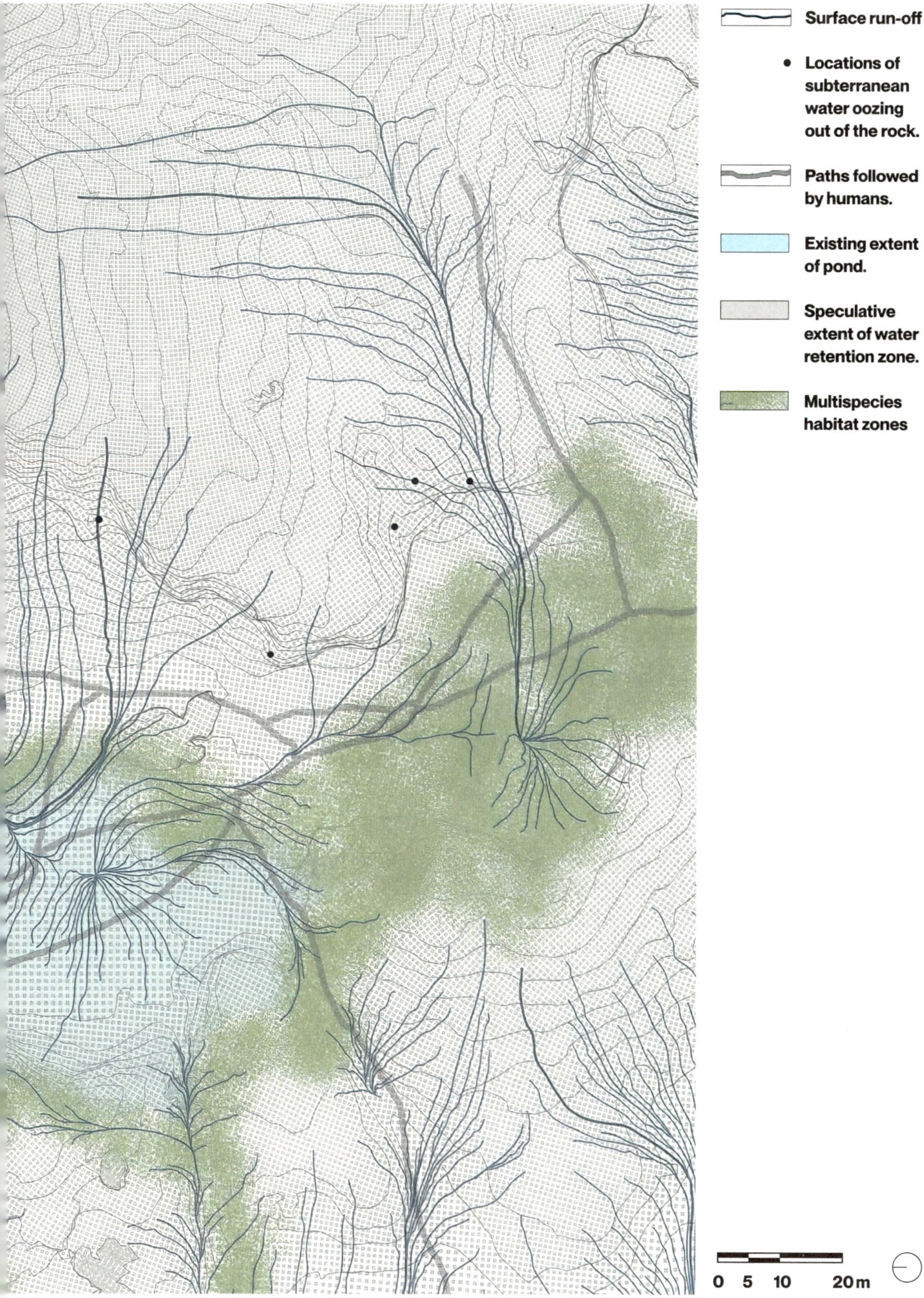
Surface run-off
Locations of subterranean water oozing out of the rock.
Paths followed by humans.
Existing extent of pond.
Speculative extent of water retention zone.
Multispecies habitat zones
0 5 10 20 m

Figure 3.19 Hybrid formation of vacancy, stone, clay, and water at the abandoned basalt quarry in Champaner, India.

The uneven vertical rock surface allows the water to accumulate in its indentations. Algae grow in such places, producing chemicals that break down the rock on which they live to access the nutrients they need. Through photosynthesis, lichens can make their own food with the available nutrients. The hybrid relation here is one of stone, water, algae, and lichens Fig 3.22. Such sites attract bees in their search for water to drink, cool their hive, and dilute honey. The vibrancy of entities such as tree roots and the vacancies of fractured rocks collaborate and collude to stabilize the assemblage of the ruin, forming a hybrid that stabilizes as it resists erosion. Similarly, the assemblage that accommodates stone, water, and algae becomes an environment for bees. The stone, algae, and water operate together in a rhizomatic manner, making an arborescence for bees and other life-forms.

Mapping Sentience directs us to ways in which a ruin's very fragility is reason for its stabilization and longevity. Contrary to architecture's ambitions for monumentality and eternal existence, fragility teaches us about the possibilities for longevity by change. It demands actions of care and repair. The sentient elementals within the assemblage self-organize to care for the fragility; each elemental, while concerned about its own stability, consolidates the assemblage into a new form. Care and repair lead to change and adaptive forms. Architectural thinking can learn from fragility, acknowledging that materials decay and decompose, focusing on making structures adaptive. Such thinking would accommodate the life of the constituent materials and anticipate how the structure can adapt once these materials begin to decay. The way forward is to design hybrid systems. For example, the architect Marco Casagrande's Ultra-Ruin (2013), in Taipei City, acknowl edges the decay of building materials such as brick and initiates a condition where a material hybrid begins to form. The disintegrating brick becomes the foundation for designing new environments for other-than-human species. Ultra-Ruin is a timber architectural organism that occupies the liminal space between terraced farms and forest. The timber structure grows out of the abandoned and decaying red brick. The use of materials and structural design ensure that the project has minimum repercussions for the existing assemblages of multispecies relationships. In this case, architecture itself enters and flourishes as a companion species in the landscape.

Conditions of Spatial Vacancies

Figure 3.20 Vegetal growth in the crack forming a hybrid at the abandoned basalt quarry in Champaner, India.

Some of the many species identified in the quarry site are *sarapanklio*, the Gujarati name for fish poison (*Tephrosia purpurea*); *kunvadiyo*, Gujarati for sickle pod (*Cassia tora*); *undhanphuli*, Gujarati for Indian borage (*Trichodesma amplexicaule Roth*), *Jodi-burumbi*, Marathi for two-flowered leucas (*Leucas biflora*); five-minute grass (*Tripogon spec*), *zinako okhrad*, Gujarati for common knotweed (*Polygonum plebeium*); *baval*, Gujarati for acacia tree (*Acacia arabica*); *saag*, Gujarati for teak (*Tectona grandis*); and *okharad*, Gujarati for purple bane (*Cyathocline purpurea*) (Chavan and Oza 1966). The gregarious *sarapanklio* is a low shrub and grows in wastelands, its purple flowers abundant in the foothills. The dry, rocky soil of the site is suitable to its growth. In turn, it provides fodder to goats that visit from nearby villages for grazing. *Kunvadiyo* is a gregarious wasteland rainy-season weed, and grows abundantly all over the hill. Birds and livestock feed on it for their protein in-

Vegetation is mostly observed on the upper portion of the quarry, creating a visible difference in the hill face—the vegetated upper part and the denuded lower half. The presence of loose soil at the top and the emerging terraces—flat surfaces that hold clay and water—cause the drastic distinction. This compels us to read the abandoned quarry as a series of spatial systems that have emerged from the distress caused when the hill was blasted. These spatial systems soon adapt to become conditions conducive to greater opportunities for multispecies habitats.

Figure 3.21 Neem tree roots intertwined with the rock forming a hybrid at the abandoned basalt quarry in Champaner, India.

take. The stone surfaces of the old fort walls nearby, as well as the rocky hill, offer an environment conducive to the growth of such gregarious herbs as *undhanphuli* and two-flowered leucas. *Undhanphuli* is a small herb that is covered with coarse hairs and has blue flowers. The two-flowered leucas is procumbent and straggling and moves along the smooth stone surface as it grows; between September and May, the area is filled with its white flowers. Five-minute grass is a perennial gregarious grass that appears abundantly in large tufts along the ledges, in cracks, on terraces, and in niches on the hill. It thrives in rocky terrain and forest margins—preferring wet rocky hillsides, steep granitic and basaltic cliffs, and boulders. The cracked hill face, with its pockets of water, is the best location for this grass.

Figure 3.22 Hybrid formation of stone, water, and algae at the abandoned basalt quarry in Champaner, India.

Vacancies created in the terrain give rise to spatial systems. Mapping vacancies identifies the factors that have led to the distress in the landscape and possibilities for regenerating the ruin from the spatial systems emerging from the decay itself. Figure 3.23 shows the various spatial typologies that have emerged from

Figure 3.23 Mapping vacancies as spatial systems at the abandoned basalt quarry in Champaner, India.

the blasting and weathering. Vacancies in the quarry have formed macroscopic caves, valleys, and steps; mesoscopic niches, terraces, and ledges; and microscopic fractures. Caves formed from the blasting are characterized by their concave nature and rugged surface **Fig 3.24**. The vacancies allow for the accumulation of material, its containment, and shelter. Valleys take shape where paths get carved out in the topography because of the continuous movement of humans and grazing cattle. These paths are further reinforced by the strong streams of surface runoff water, which give the paths a smooth curvilinear form **Fig 3.25**. Niches emerged on the cliff face from the impact of pieces of broken stone hitting the rock face during blasting. Consequently, in these niches, clay gets deposited over time because of water runoff, providing an environment conducive to other species **Fig 3.26**. Steps with well-defined rectilinear edges were identified in the terrain, another spatial typology that has emerged from blasting, which caused the stone to break along the lines of its structural weakness. **Fig 3.27** Similar to steps but larger, terraces were formed on the cliff face as a result of blasting. Ledges are horizontal projections that receive clay particles carried by erosion, becoming microhabitats for various plant species and serving as an example of a spatial system that fosters multispecies habitats. **Fig 3.28**

Fractures or cracks are crucial for determining the weak zones in the cliff face, **Fig 3.29** allowing for the accumulation of clay particles and water, which supports plant growth. These maps illustrate the vacancies created from drilling and blasting at a macro scale. These concave formations are characterized by an absence of sharp corners or edges; the vertical plane gently undulates, rendering a seamless surface.

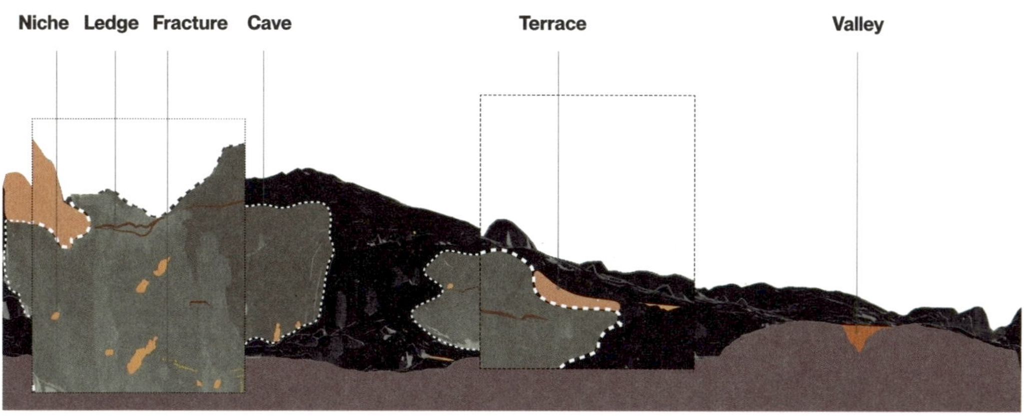

Figure 3.24 Cave as a spatial typology of vacancy at the abandoned basalt quarry in Champaner, India.

Figure 3.25 Path as a spatial typology of vacancy at the abandoned basalt quarry in Champaner, India.

Figure 3.26 Niche as a spatial typology of vacancy at the abandoned basalt quarry in Champaner, India.

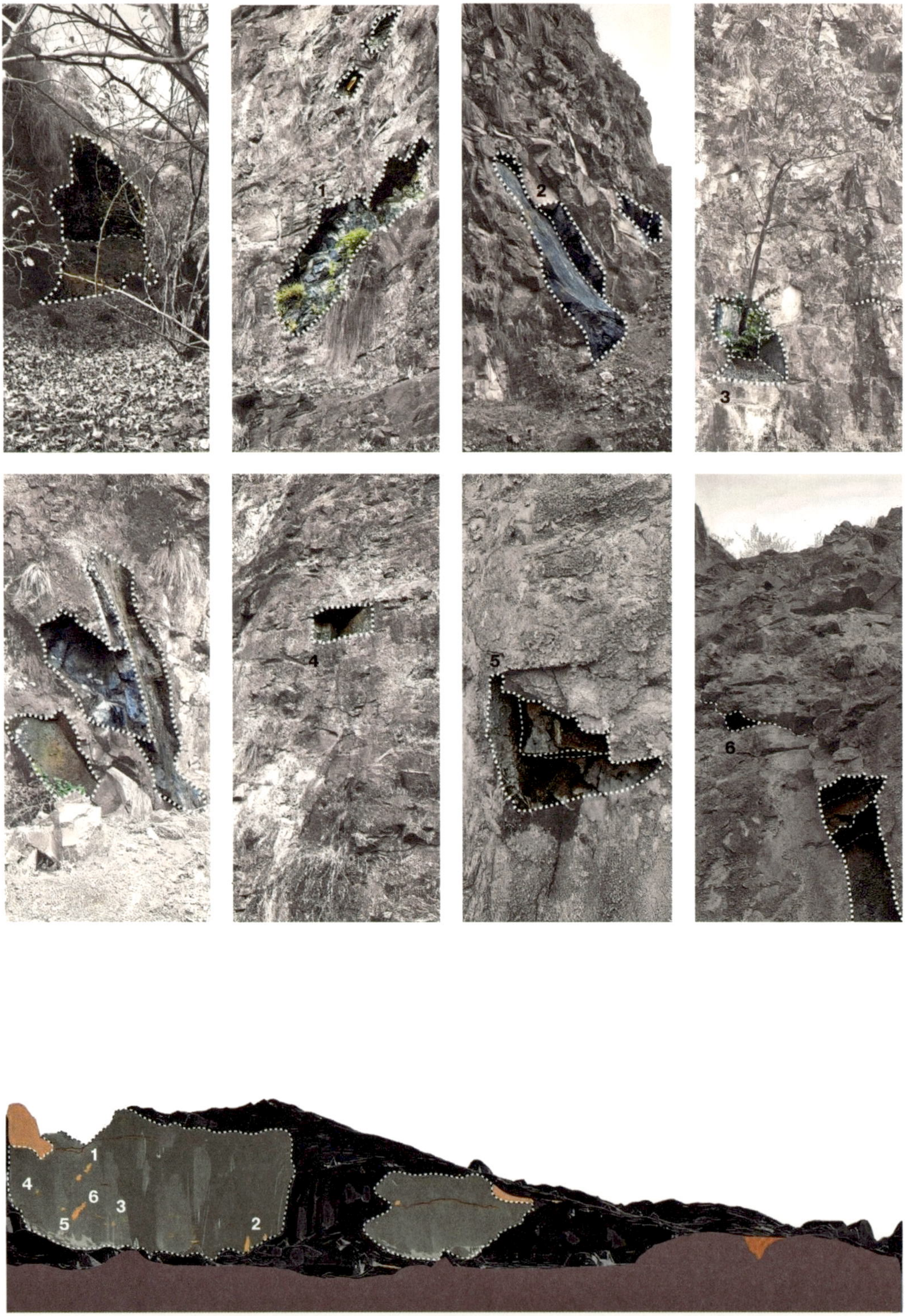

Figure 3.27 Step as a spatial typology of vacancy at the abandoned basalt quarry in Champaner, India.

Figure 3.28 Ledge as a spatial typology of vacancy at the abandoned basalt quarry in Champaner, India.

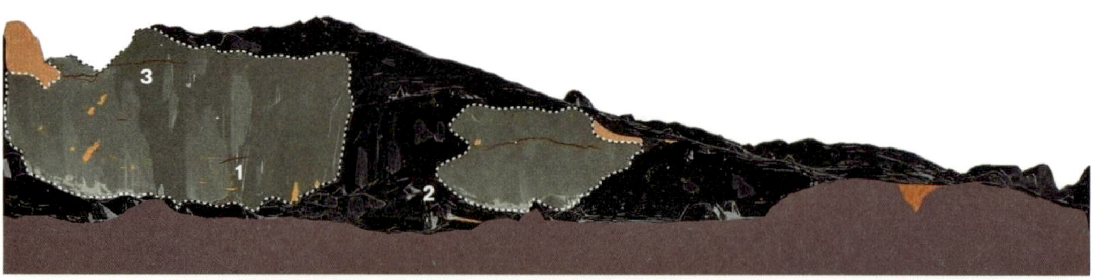

Figure 3.29 Crack as a spatial typology of vacancy at the abandoned basalt quarry in Champaner, India.

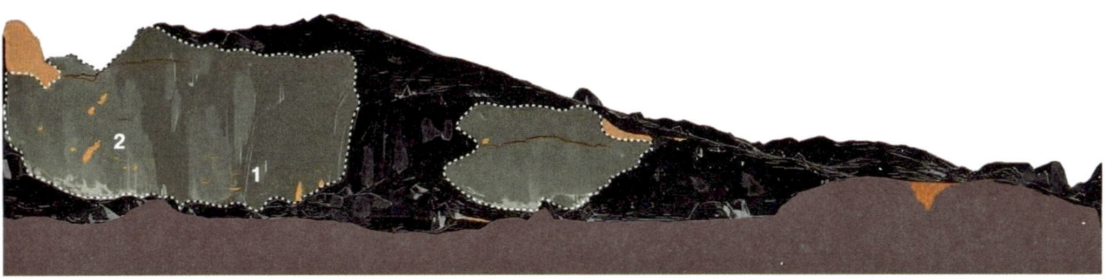

Vacancies can accommodate architectural built forms. Mapping Sentience is a reminder to architects of not just Haraway's tentacular thinking but also the potential of prosthetics as a design intervention. As in the mills discussed above, surfaces act as armatures for vegetation. Jamie North created a work where native Australian plant species are allowed to grow in the interstitial spaces of decaying industrial composites of concrete and reinforcement bars. North's work points to the ability of discarded materials to forge kinships between human and nonhuman entities. It shows that materials considered ruins or waste, when amalgamated in a specific form and favorable conditions, can become thresholds between the human and nonhuman. Similarly, the architectural studio R&Sie(n)'s *I'm Lost in Paris* (2008) creates an urban incongruity by introducing dense vegetation into the site and surface of a building in the French capital, forming a physical space of "becoming-with" between the plants and the building. Its metal armature and handcrafted glass bulbs create a hydroponic environment for the growth of ferns. This prosthetic armature enables architecture (and architectural elements) to become-with the nonhuman agents on and around the site. This relation is not limited to the fern, as the growth of one species leads to a flourishing ecological system. The built form here loses its singularity as an objectin the urban landscape and becomes a companion species.

Persistent Queering

Ruins are witness to, accommodate, and accentuate a response-ability in their inhabitants. In the continuous movement of energy and materials initiated and sustained by erosion, the ruins become spatially receptive. Essentially, the response-ability of the elemental components is evident in their movement. They move in order to stabilize. To stabilize means to find shelter. To stabilize also means to find an adequate source of nourishment. The weight of components of the ruins, such as rocks, water, and vegetation roots, respond to gravity, following a path that allows them to balance and stabilize, causing deposits and sedimentation. To stabilize also means to be safe, to take paths away from danger. Not every condition is conducive to proliferation, as conditions that cause harm are skipped or avoided, leading to a different set of relationships. For example, the squirrel steers clear of overgrown bushes to avoid any dangers that may be inside. The surfaces of the ruin are available to rodents and birds while unavailable to life-forms such as humans; the dilapidated walls make space for nesting and roosting while temperature, moisture, and surrounding vegetation create favorable conditions for nonhuman habitats. Trees at Pickers Mill make kin with the remnants of the broken north-light truss to create a canopy. The roots of the tree entangle with the wall, finding a way through the weakened mortar and clasping onto the bricks to consolidate the vertical surface. The broken wall is no longer weak because the entangling roots strengthen it. A new hybrid is thus formed, consisting of the living roots and the inanimate brick and mortar. The parts of the wall that do not participate in the hybrid fall away. This hybrid—a cyborg—demonstrates the importance of interdependency in order to survive. Mapping Sentience in the ruin reveals it as an assemblage of hybrids—combining human-made elements in a continuous state of morphing when open to surrounding life-forms. The human-made is hence not separated from the nonhuman or "natural." Human-made elements such as walls and roofs at the NC Mill or the blasted rock at the quarry are hybrids. The wall is not just a wall but a hybrid of wall, roots, and squirrels, etc., while the roof is a hybrid of the metal frame, growing stems, falling leaves, monkeys, and asbestos. Ecofeminist philosopher Val Plumwood and anthropologists Haraway and Arturo Escobar are among the many thinkers who have discussed that a pristine form of nature does not exist but a mutating relationship between nature and culture does exist, in which both continuously affect and change one another (Plumwood 1993; Haraway 2016; Escobar 1999).

Metal beams and trusses—remnants of the erstwhile mills—act like prosthetics of the ruins. Creepers and other vegetation cling onto them and grow. A prosthetic limb attached to a human body works in unison with the body but always retains its component features. Similarly, in the ruin, the metal armatures become overgrown with vegetation, and continue to extend that support if the armatures can maintain their fundamental characteristics. Human prosthetics are designed to support a certain weight. Similarly, the prosthetics in the ruins last as long as the weight of the supporting life-forms does not overpower them. Prosthetics are different from hybrids in their resistance to mutation—the individual properties do not change—which is why they appear as remnants of a support system for a body—the mill building—that has lived its life and is now available to support something else.

The grass genus *Tripogon* flourishes on the ledges of the basalt quarry. *Tripogon* is derived from the Greek *treis* (three) and *pogon* (beard), and refers to three apical awns and three basal hair tufts. Awns, a distinct morphological and physiological characteristic of grass, are bristle-like extensions from the lemma that enclose the grass floret. Awns assist in seed dispersal, germination, and photosynthesis. They effectively self-cultivate by drilling themselves into the soil. They follow a pumping movement in a diurnal environment that alternates between high and low humidity. When humidity rises, the awns become erect, draw together, and push the plant into the soil; when humidity drops, the awns slacken but take the form of a ratchet hook and hold on to the soil. Awns also become entangled with passing animals, who disperse them. As Haraway writes, "The tentacular are not disembodied figures; they are [...] fibrous entities, flagellated beings,

[...] fungal tangles, probing creepers, swelling roots, reaching and climbing tendrilled ones" (Haraway 2016b, 32). The awns make the grass tentacular, creating attachments and detachments. As it finds shelter in rock crevices and moves along available surfaces, the grass feels its way to situate itself, weaving networks with passing animals. It participates in what Haraway calls "making cuts and knots," in initiating "consequences but not determinisms" (Haraway 2016b, 31). The grass awn latches onto unknown animals, dispersing itself, allowing itself a greater opportunity for survival. The root knotting with the loose rock results in a shared stabilization of both the rock and the tree. It does not know where and how it will end up; it is open to possibilities. These acts of detachment and attachment are acts in which participants adapt, morph into hybrids, move, make new alliances, and therefore cultivate response-ability. They are an outcome of an ongoing practice of "collective knowing and doing" (Haraway 2016b, 34).

The inhabiting life-forms adapt the place to their needs, which in turn leads to a renewal and decomposition of the ruin. In this constant renewal, the site mutates. Conditions of ruination become necessary conditions for renewal. The site witnesses a continuous cycle of new and emerging hybrids that mutate into new hybrids. In this hybridization, new energies and strengths are forged that combine the collective strength of its constituting elements. The site then becomes a container of many hybrids—which are already on their way to becoming new hybrids—never determinable, sometimes precarious, and always dependent on their ability and will to thrive. This ability of the ruin to adapt makes it queer. The elementals adapting into hybrids exhibit characteristics of shifting, transforming, or evolving to survive within the dynamic ruin. Queering means to evade norms, whether those of identity, sexuality, or societal roles; and embrace transformation. Both processes resist fixed categories and embrace change and non-conformity. Ruin is accommodative, inclusive, and allows for several life-forms to exercise their specificity and identity.

These are the "partial connections" that conjugate the various worlds of animate and inanimate existence in the ruins (Haraway 2016b, 13). There are no universal patterns except the persistent queering, relying on a constant morphing of interdependencies. The ruin is an open-ended opportunity for collaborative survival. It makes space for unexpected interspecies alliances. On the way to stabilization, it is a "recuperating pluriverse" (Haraway 2016b, 11). The ruin is sentient; it is a terrapolis. Mapping Sentience in these ruins calls for a need to imagine architectural as well as non-architectural elementals as hybrids in order to foster cohabitative living.

4 Ecotone Architecture – Articulations of Posthumanist Elemental Assemblages

Ruins are sites of interdependence and cohabitation of organic and inorganic elements. Mapping Sentience identifies existing and emerging conditions that enable these interdependencies. This mapping reveals the spatial and physical parameters that allow multispecies growth. Surface irregularities, the ability to hold moisture, the temperature, and vegetation's proximity to wall surfaces are some such parameters—traditionally considered detrimental to the longevity of architecture, they appear to contribute to multispecies habitats. To further an agenda that prioritizes these habitats, it becomes imperative for architects to treat each site as an assmblage composed of entities, territories, and processes. As discussed in Chapter 2, these entities are in a persistent state of interaction with other proximate entities, maintaining constant deterritorializations and reterritorializations and blurring the boundaries of assemblages.

The following six architectural lessons learned from Mapping Sentience can be used to imagine architectures for ecological recovery projects. These lessons necessitate a consideration and accommodation of the mapping parameters outlined in Chapter 3, which are absent in traditional architectural thinking.

First, every site can be read in a tentacular manner. To intervene architecturally in a site requires acknowledging existing entities, identifying the territories they occupy, and entering those ongoing processes. Entities are species such as squirrels, bees, birds, monkeys, cryptogams, plants, trees, and matter such as decaying bricks, dried leaves, soil, and moisture. Territories are spatial vacancies such as hollows in tree trunks, cracks in the rock surface, and cliff ledges. Reading the site in a tentacular manner is a subversion of the conventional practice of architecture, where a site is seen as a tabula rasa, or merely a set of topographical features. Mapping Sentience reveals that elements traverse a ruin following a tentacular feeling of the surfaces. Finding vacancies in which to nestle and finding surfaces on which to step is part of a tentacular reading of a milieu for placing an architectural form.

Second, prioritize the receptivity of irregular surfaces over the conventional preference for smooth sterilized surfaces. The former are essential for retaining moisture and allowing dust to settle, patinas to grow, and algae to proliferate—in other words, forms of contamination. Contamination brings a milieu closer to a multispecies habitat than an exclusively human habitat. Diverse species thrive in the ruin by forming a habitat within discarded elements and on moist, dirty surfaces. The ruinous brick surface and the moisture on it are the drivers of patina growth. In architectural thinking, contaminants need to be critically assessed from a human perspective for their potential to host nonhuman life-forms.

Third, prioritize the indeterminacy of the architectural form over the conventional preference for form-based objects of architecture. In an assemblage, indeterminacy is one of the main producers of living systems. To make space for uncertainty within the built form, the architect shares agency to shape the built form and its surroundings with other existing life-forms and entities over time. This subverts the conventional architectural notion of giving sole agency to the designer and the human residents.

Fourth, prioritize architecture as part of a network of human and nonhuman elements. The proximity between a tree and a wall enables interspecies movements, such as squirrels and birds searching for food and shelter. Here, architectural design not only creates new networks but also sustains the networks already present on the site, which are read through tentacular thinking. This subverts the conventional architectural practice of placing trees as landscape elements and walls as part of a distinct structural composition.

Fifth, prioritize hybrid forms and systems in architecture as catalysts for multispecies cohabitation. As explored in Chapter 1, the animate and inanimate elements collaborate to stabilize the assemblage of ruins. Through this process, hybrid systems emerge and aim for stability. The sentient components of the assemblage self-organize to repair fragilities; while each element focuses on its own stability. In this way, care and repair foster transformation and adaptability. Architectural thinking can draw inspiration from this by embracing fragility and acknowledging the inevitability of decay. As materials break down and decompose, architecture can channel its efforts into creating structures that are adaptive and responsive to change. Such a thinking would accommodate the life of constituent materials and anticipate how the structure can adapt once the materials begin to decay. The way forward would be to design hybrid systems.

Sixth, prioritize architectural inserts as prosthetics in adaptive reuse projects. Mapping Sentience reveals that the various participating life-forms use the physical environment of the ruin as a prosthetic— sometimes as an external support and sometimes as an inherent structural support. In both cases, the life-forms, once stabilized and strong enough, abandon the prosthetic; however, the prosthetic remains, providing support to other life-forms. For example, the peepal tree in the New Commercial Mill (NC Mill) ruin grows onto the disintegrating brick wall to stabilize itself, and over time it stabilizes the wall as well. This observation directs us to design architectural systems that have a prosthetic quality—an element that inserts itself into a site to heal a broken ecology. This is useful in establishing linkages and relationships between various spatial resources at a given site. Prosthetics is a useful way of treating architectural interventions in adaptive reuse projects or rejuvenation projects, such as Casagrande's Treasure Hill (2003).

The following is a survey of contemporary architectural projects and techniques that foster, or have the potential to foster, multispecies architecture. The examples range from built to speculative, temporary installations to permanent structures, vernacular to adaptive reuse.

Tentacular Architecture

Jingkieng Jri, or the living root bridges, in the West Jaintia Hills and East Khasi Hills districts of the northeast state of Meghalaya, are an example of tentacular architecture. They are suspension bridges made from live plant roots, spanning raised stream banks that run through dense forests. The aerial roots of rubber fig trees (*Ficus elastica*) easily anchor themselves to steep slopes and rocky surfaces. Hence, when the roots are directed across the streambeds horizontally, they quickly take hold on the opposite side. The roots then shorten, thicken, and produce more roots, which are similarly trained (Ludwig et al. 2019, 1). The living root bridges take ten to fifteen years to take shape and strengthen. The strength of the living root bridges increases with age as the roots keep growing. As long as the host tree remains healthy, the roots that form the bridge will continue to thicken and strengthen; hence, the bridge continues to self-renew and self-strengthen. The living root bridges are testimony to the collaborative potential of the botanical and the human in creating robust structures that continue to strengthen with age. Almost two hundred years ago, the Khasis directed rubber tree roots through the hollowed trunks of Areca palm (*catechu*) from either side of a stream to meet midway across the waterway. The roots were then tended with great care until they grew long and strong enough to reach the opposite bank. In the process, the roots intertwined with one another, strengthening further, and increasing their capacity to hold the weight of humans. This practice has since continued. The Khasi and Jaintia communities hand-sculpt the pliable aerial roots of the rubber tree. The young roots are encouraged to inosculate by intertwining, leading to dense interwoven frame-work-like structures (Ludwig et al. 2019, 1). Sticks, stones, and other objects are used to stabilize the growing bridge. Continuous hand-sculpting is needed to prune the roots in order to strengthen the bridge. The bridges are made more complex with the addition of handrails or an upper story, using the same strategy of directing roots in the desired direction. **Fig 4.1**

This method is not limited to these bridges but is also used to make ladders, platforms, towers, steps, and structures to prevent erosion and landslides (UNESCO 2022). The living root bridges embody a wide spectrum of structural typologies, resembling characteristics of suspension bridges, cable-stayed bridges, arches, trusses, and simply supported beams (Ludwig et al. 2019, 1). The secondary shoots from the longer roots on the upper level are tied around and grown into the roots beneath them, acting simultaneously as a handrail and a suspending chain, while the lower roots act as a footway. Other roots are interlaced to form a ladder to provide access to the bridge from the bank (Yule 1844, 613).

Figure 4.1 Two-story living root bridges in Nongriat, India.

The practice of making these bridges was first recorded in 1844 by Henry Yule, a Scottish geographer. At that time, some of the bridges spanned a length of ninety feet (Yule 1844, 613), signifying that the practice had been around for many years. The "Living Root Bridges Cultural Landscape" has been on UNESCO's Tentative List for World Heritage since February 2022. The list recognizes 72 living root bridges connecting as many as 75 villages in Meghalaya. Most of the bridges are found growing between 50 and 1,150 meters above sea level in subtropical moist broadleaf forests on steep hillsides. Today, some of the bridges are 100 feet long and can hold up to 50 people at once.

In certain places, the living root bridges are conceived as hybrid forms. Near the village of Nongriat, rubber tree roots have been trained across a pre-existing steel wire bridge to form a hybrid structure. Here, the steel structure forms a scaffold on which the roots grow and move along to form the bridge. With the strengthening of the roots, the steel wires are becoming redundant and will be allowed to rust away. The steel structure, in this case, acts as a prosthetic supporting the young roots until they gain strength. The steel structure remains relevant until the bridge becomes solely dependent on the living roots.

Recently, this technique has been developed and adopted in architecture. For example, Baubotanik architecture, coined by Ferdinand Ludwig in 2007, uses living trees as a load-bearing structural system (Oommen 2015). It is a construction method that combines technical joints and plant growth. The living and nonliving elements are intertwined to grow together, forming plant-metal hybrids. Over time, as trees age, the joints and living elements start to fuse, increasing the strength of the structural connections. The plant exhibits its own characteristics, as does the metal structure—together, they form a structural system that increases its strength as time passes. The dynamically evolving relationship between the plant and the human-made joint, which aims for mutual longevity, makes this an assemblage. Baubotanik buildings will take years to form and over time they start to become part of the ecology of their surroundings.

Receptive Architecture

Historically, the primary function of walls has been to provide protection from the environment. Over time, they have become an element of division, distancing humans from their environment. The architect Joyce Hwang's 2015 project Habitat Wall inverts this phenomenon by creating walls where more-than-human species such as birds and bats can reside. Here, instead of acting as a separation, the wall becomes a receptive element. Bats play an important role in the pollination of over 250 plant species (Fleming et al. 2009, 1017) and therefore are vital for the ecosystem as well as food production. They are an facing an increased risk of extinction owing to habitat loss. Hwang's project, similar to this book, was born from concerns of widespread urban species loss.

The first step in Habitat Wall was understanding the necessary conditions for bat and bird habitats. Along with crevice-like spaces to roost in, bats also prefer spaces that retain warmth and have textured surfaces to anchor on. Taking these requirements into consideration, Hwang built a wall prototype from cedar, pine, and disused building materials, with crevices for habitat creation. A series of wooden planks of different heights are sandwiched together to create these crevices; the form of the openings makes the wall receptive to bats. Recycled materials such as timber and old window shutters and doors provide textured surfaces that enable bats to climb into the cavities. The stacking of the wooden surfaces also retains the warmth absorbed from the sun during the day, providing better insulation, and a thermal consistency that is crucial for their dwellings. Habitat Wall also has proper conditions for cliff-dwelling birds to roost and nesting boxes for birds on its surface. **Fig 4.2**

With Habitat Wall, designed as a part of human habitat, Hwang makes architecture an interface, a threshold between the human and other species. The same element protects human habitation and creates space for nonhuman species to take agency and create a habitat. Furthermore, the use of recycled and disused material suggests the circular movement of matter through our environment, where the waste of one species becomes the habitat for another.

As observed in the sentient mappings of the NC Mill, one of the main drivers of vegetal growth on the wall surfaces of the building is moisture retention, which creates substrata for hosting moss species. The second key driver is surface irregularity and modulation. The Poikilohydric Living Walls (PLW) project, developed by Marcos Cruz together with Richard Beckett, Sandra Manso Blanco, and Brenda Parker from 2014 to 2020, prioritizes contamination through irregular surfaces that are receptive to the biological growth of poikilohydric cryptogamic species such as moss, algae, and fungi. Poikilohydric species can regulate their photosynthesis activity depending on water availability. The unique structural and physiological capacity of these species enables them to resist lengthy drought periods and extreme temperatures. PLW integrates these self-regulated biological systems with urban infrastructures without the need for additional irrigation and maintenance (Cruz 2022, 10). To increase photosynthetic activity and retain water for prolonged periods of time, Cruz and his team designed cementitious material substrates with specific surface morphologies derived from studying tree barks. PLW is therefore a receptive interface that receives and holds water for cryptogams to grow.

Figure 4.2 Habitat Wall prototype incorporating living spaces for birds and bats by Joyce Hwang.

These walls offer an interface for the material-tectonic-environmental negotiations between human and nonhuman (Birch 2016). In imagining architecture as a bark, PLW sustain life through their own thickness and material substrata. The wall surface is a manifestation of a “becoming-with” the vegetation. This becoming-with involves an empathetic understanding of the needs of the nonhuman poikilohydric cryptogam habitat. PLW acknowledges the growth cycles of cryptogams and does not promote a year-round green facade. When cryptogams “gradually stain” the surfaces, they signal that the surfaces are “alive and active contributors to the environment” (Cruz 2022, 10). The uncertain and irregular growth on the facade contradicts the sense of clarity, cleanliness, and geometry that is usually desired by architects. It embraces the indeterminacy of plant growth, treating it as an opportunity for redefining facade aesthetics and urging a fresh perspective on the aesthetics of contamination. In envisaging PLW specifically for aging buildings (Cruz 2022, 10), the project subverts the conventional architectural idea that buildings have to look the same. It embraces impurity and hybridity derived from self-regulated cryptogams that grow on aging bioreceptive surfaces.[1] Accommodating cryptograms on facades comes with both tectonic and aesthetic challenges.

1 A bioreceptive material can be inhabited by living organisms without it necessarily undergoing any form of biodeterioration.

Architecture of Indeterminacy

Ruin Garden (2019), by the architect Tanja Lincke and the artist Anselm Reyle, works with the indeterminacy and precarity of architectural elements cohabitating with plant growth. The project transformed a former shipyard building in Berlin. Among the dilapidated buildings on the site, the former boathouse building was the largest, offering no possibilities for reuse. Instead of demolishing it, the architects decided to open it up by taking away the roof, multiple walls, and parts of the flooring, thereby creating the possibility of plant growth. Piles of concrete slabs removed from the building were strewn across the site. These concrete surfaces, due to their unevenness and capacity to retain moisture, create conditions conducive to moss and other plant growth. These slabs echo the artwork of Jamie North, who uses hostile abandoned materials—left over from colonization, industrialization, or agriculture—to grow native Australian plant species. Similarly, in the Ruin Garden, the use of concrete, brick, and rebars reveals how ruined materials can forge kinship between human and nonhuman entities. The remains of concrete flooring make way for tall grass like echinacea and phlox, moving away from symmetric and manicured lawn landscapes. It shows that materials termed ruins or waste, when amalgamated in a specific form and favorable conditions, can become thresholds between the human and nonhuman. Fig 4.3

Figure 4.3 Indeterminate vegetal growth at Tanja Lincke Architekten's Ruin Garden, Berlin.

The Ruin Garden demonstrates two types of indeterminacies. The first is the indeterminacy demonstrated by the building materials in changing their inherent characteristics when exposed to atmospheric conditions: the growth of plants over and around the floor and wall surfaces continuously changes the attributes of the material. The second is the uncertainty propelled by a lack of functional specificity. The adaptable natural space can be used for diverse functions at different times of the year. With this step, the project also questions architecture's obsession with assigning specific functions to certain spaces. The design makes space for an indeterminacy that creates conditions conducive to plants having agency and making a habitat. The project is never complete, as the dwellers continuously adapt to and become-with the other species cohabitating in the garden. The Ruin Garden is a step toward reimagining architectural form, function, and material to support human–plant cohabitation.

The traditional focus of architecture on determinacy—be it of form, function, or the response of material over time—conflicts with multispecies cohabitation, as species growth and interaction do not have fixed parameters. At the same time, making space for unforeseen interactions among species does not mean a complete loss of control over a space, but rather a sharing of control. Such sharing is visible in the Ruin Garden. The removal of floor and wall material allows for plants to grow, while humans participate further by pruning and trimming the growth.

Architecture of Networks

The project Human-Critter Block, proposed by Jaikishore A. at a ruinous site in the urban precinct of Qaiserbagh, is imagined as an architecture of networks.[2] Qaiserbagh was constructed in the 1840s as part of a royal palace for Nawab Wajid Ali Shah. Remembered as a site that empowered women socially, culturally, financially, and politically, it was designed with the urban ecological parameters of the time (Mithal and Paul 2024, 105, 120–29). However, after the 1857 war of independence and subsequent takeover of the property by the British, it became a site of colonial oppression and was destroyed by colonial town-planning interventions. Today, Qaiserbagh is a busy urban setting consisting

2 The project is part of Sonal Mithal's studio "Staging Ecologies: Politics of Gender and Memory in the Recovery of Qaiserbagh, Lucknow, India," offered at CEPT University in spring 2023.

of historical structures either occupied by residents or lying abandoned. Some of these properties have undergone severe decay owing to human neglect after conflicts over ownership and financial limitations. Using the specificity of this area, the Human-Critter Block responded to the call to reframe the scope of architecture and imagine inventive ways of addressing gender, memory, and ecology as central concerns for a sustainable Indian city.

Similar to the squirrel mapping at the NC Mill discussed in the previous chapter, Jaikishore closely followed and mapped the movements of squirrels in Qaiserbagh. In Jaikishore's reading, squirrels and other swift critters use the network of electric posts and wires for their movement. He mapped the electric posts to understand how they shaped the squirrels' paths for maneuvering above busy roads and accessing surrounding trees. He then mapped the ruined facades in relation to the movement of squirrels and the location of their nests. The mapping revealed how the specific conditions of the materiality of the facade—such as Lakhori bricks (thinner and wider bricks used during nawabi times), British bricks, plaster, and moss formation—were conducive to squirrels' day-to-day activities. A ruined facade experiences a high volume of squirrel activity. The animals prefer to use the Lakhori bricks to climb because they are thin, while they make nests in small crevices in the British bricks, as they are relatively taller and form deeper and bigger niches. **Fig 4.4**

Jaikishore derived an architectural design manifesto from these mappings that focused on achieving multispecies inclusivity by foregrounding differing degrees of overlaps. These overlaps are present between the newly made and the ruined, the human-made and the nonhuman-made, the human-occupied space and the nonhuman-occupied space. Rather than "providing" for nonhumans, the project finds, architects should initiate conditions that enable nonhumans to cohabit with humans. The project considers synanthropic species such as squirrels and barn swallows (mapped in the introductory chapter of this book) that benefit from human-made structures and activities, consequently attaining a symbiotic relationship among the various species.

The manifesto is demonstrated in a small retrofit project with no specific program, Human-Critter Block, which was later developed into a programmatic building, the almond processing plant. The retrofit was inserted into the part of a ruined structure where the only part of the ground floor that remains are the walls. The overlap between the newly built and the ruined becomes a space for squirrel habitation while also stabilizing the

Figure 4.4 Squirrel activity on a ruined brick wall at Qaiserbagh in Lucknow, India.

Nesting on british bricks

Lakhauri bricks ma-jorly used for climbing

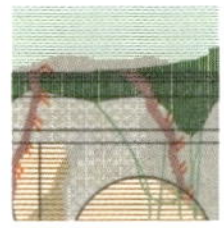

Cracks on facade are used for climbing

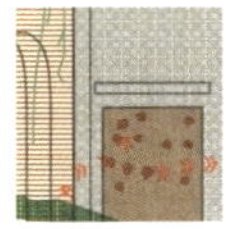

Holes for dead ends not used for nesting

Ledges aid in movement on smooth surfaces

Stems and vines used for climbing

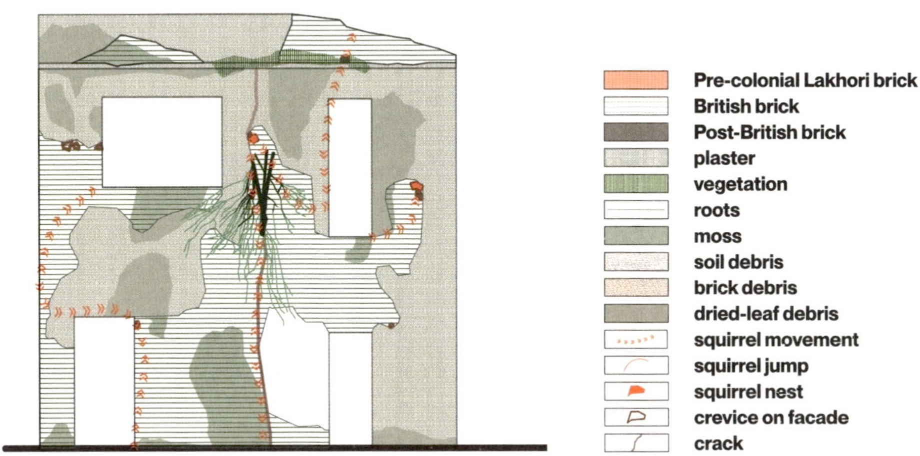

fragilities of the ruined structure. The three-story facade of the ruined structure, along with the ground-floor walls, are made part of the retrofit, and squirrels are allowed to enter the retrofit enclosure via the ruined walls that form part of the proposed interior. On the ground floor, humans can partially witness the squirrel activities, but once they reach the first floor they can see their complete activities. This is made possible by a careful play of volumes. Light metal rods supporting the retrofit form an framework independent from the ruin. Existing lintels of openings in walls and existing slabs are reinforced by steel members, thus stabilizing the ruin. The newly designed soffits of window sunshades are paneled with aged wood for barn swallows to nest. The droppings produced by these swallow colonies fertilize the planter boxes on the first floor and add to the organic matter for the compost pit on the ground floor.

Though Jaikishore imagined the retrofit as an indeterminate space in terms of functionality, he extends it using an adjoining abandoned residence to demonstrate the ability of such retrofits and multispecies environments to become programmatic spaces. The almond processing facility activates a system of agricultural production for humans that will also benefit the other species that exist in the space. In this facility, the by-products of the harvested crop will be used either by humans or the surrounding nonhumans—in this case, squirrels, who eat the nuts along with their shells. The design philosophy seeks to promote environmental sustainability by adopting a cyclic approach to the design, where resources are efficiently utilized and waste products minimized. Almonds are cultivated in a fully controlled environment on the first floor. The by-products are taken to dedicated compartments to be used by squirrels or to other cogeneration facilities. The building is envisaged as a greenhouse, organically shaped to retain the existing mature trees on the site. Ethylene tetrafluoroethylene (ETFE) panels are used instead of glass to reduce heat transmission while ensuring better light transmission. A biome is created on the east side as a buffer from the road and to provide shade for visitors, who move along on a ramp. The majority of the first floor allows visitors to observe the inner workings of the project. The ramps are 2.4 meters higher than the plane of cultivation in order to maintain an unobstructed view for the visitors. A separator, introduced on the conveyor belts, punctures the ruined wall to ensure that squirrels don't intrude into the factory's working space. The receiving area collects the harvested almonds. In addition to almonds (*Prunus dulcis*), carandas (*Carissa carandas*), and peaches (*Prunus persica*) could also be grown here. Crops relevant to the history of Qaiserbagh help recall the decolonial history of the site. Fig 4.5

Figure 4.5 **Retrofit in a ruined structure allowing a space for squirrel habitation.**

Section AA' of retrofit

Plan of retrofit

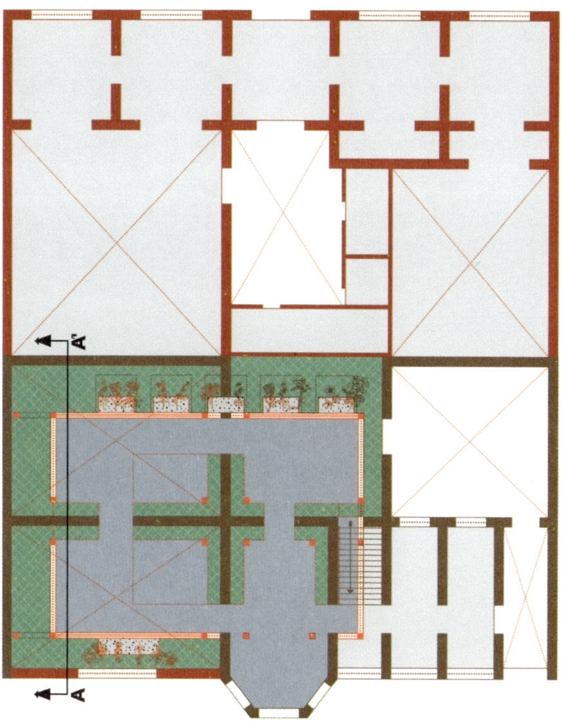

Detail of human and squirrel circulation in the almond processing facility

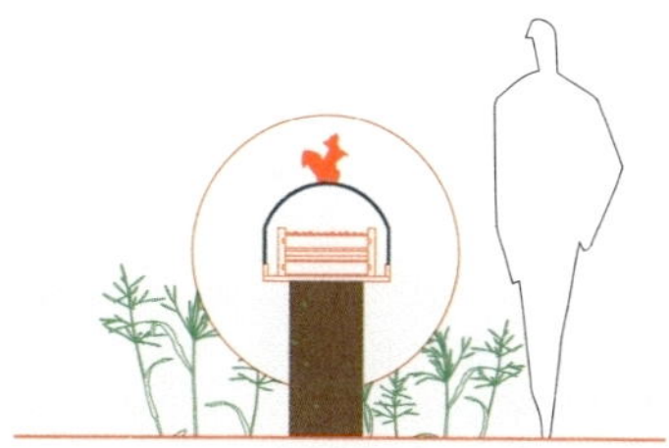

Detail of human and squirrel circulation in the almond processing facility

The Garden House (2013–ongoing) by Baracco+Wright Architects, located on Boonwurrung land in southeastern Australia, is an example of architecture that sensitively places itself in the ecological networks of the site and becomes part of them. The project site has a layered natural history. It is a heavily vegetated area between cleared grazing lands. It depicts the landscape that existed prior to the habitation of humans and domesticated animals in the region. Over time, patches of endemic vegetation, tea-tree heath, mown grass, introduced species, and plants considered invasive weeds have taken over this vegetative area. **Fig 4.6**

Figure 4.6 Plan and section showing the placement and interaction between architecture and surrounding vegetation at Baracco+Wright Architects' Garden House, Westernport, Australia.

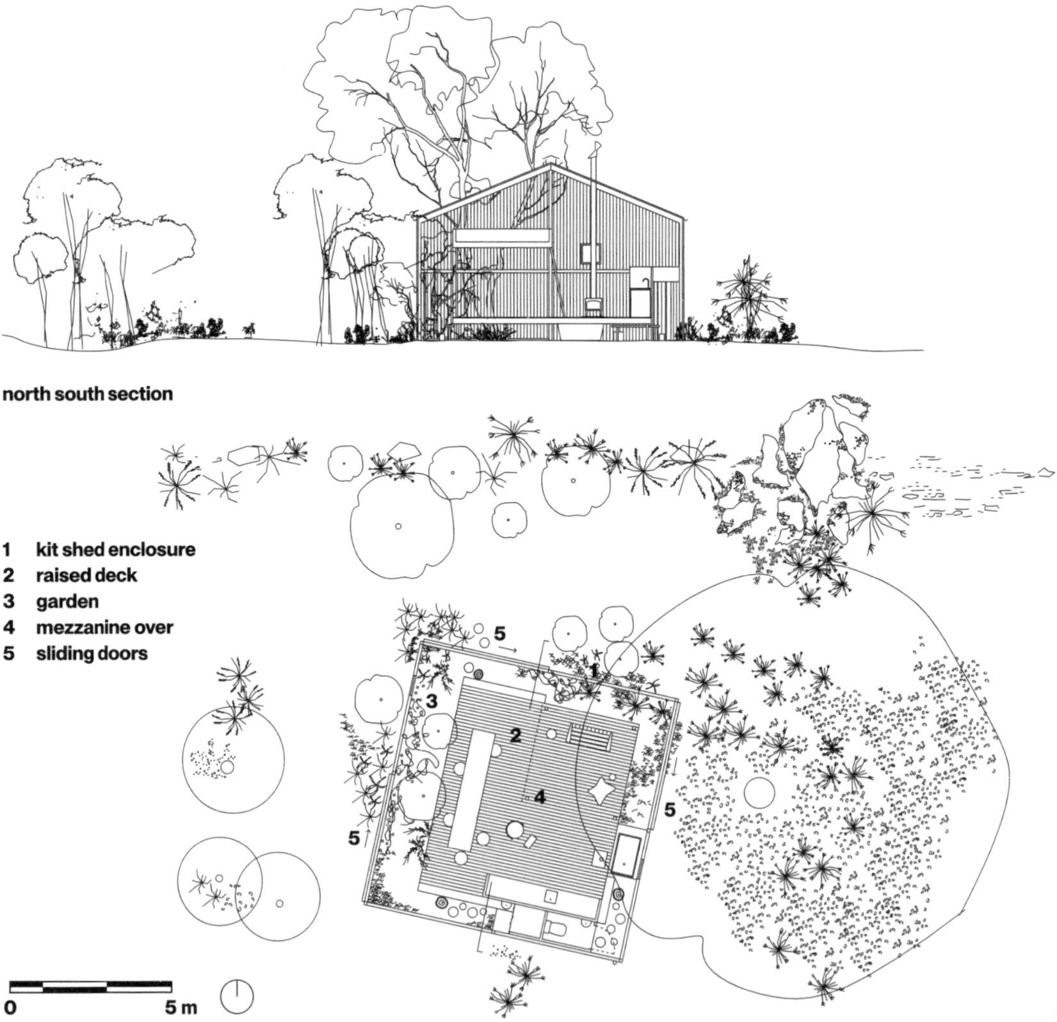

The architects carried out an extensive reading of the landscape to consider the significance of native vegetation on the site, which incorporated not just what plant species are endemic to the site but also their symbiotic relationships with the surrounding vegetation and their habitat requirements. The architects learned that the existence of endemic terrestrial orchids indicated the presence of unaltered soil. Greenhood orchids (*Pterostylis nutans*) have a symbiotic relationship with certain trees and require mycorrhizal fungi for their germination, which acts as a communication network for various trees.

An architectural intervention in such an ecologically rich and sensitive environment could potentially change the hydrology of the land; water penetration, overland flow, microclimate, and tree removal would cause the orchids to disappear. Hence, a suitable placement for the intervention was the biggest challenge. The project investigated ways to repair and regenerate endemic species growth. To support and strengthen the remaining indigenous vegetation, the architects used the Bradley method, which involves clearing weeds around healthy patches of native vegetation so that each area can be taken over by the regeneration of native plants that replace the weeds (AABR 2023). The Bradley method revealed an area that was not regenerating, which is where the Garden House was placed—on a raised platform to minimally interfere with existing interspecies relationships. To ensure that the house sat lightly, the architects used thin sections of steel and handmade timber. To ensure translucence, they used polycarbonate sheets for the walls.

The walls facilitate a connection with the surroundings, making the Garden House in and of the environment. Instead of the traditional separators such as walls, windows, rooms, and floors, vegetation on both sides of the polycarbonate sheets creates a soft boundary. Along with this vertical porosity, there is also horizontal porosity, as the ground surfaces are left unsealed and an elevated floor is created from wood. This floor is offset from the polycarbonate walls, creating both a threshold and a space for species and floodwaters to move through. The building's presence does not hinder the movement of other natural elements through the site. **Fig 4.7** Along with the visual porosity, there is also aural porosity, as one can hear the noises of nature. According to Louise Wright, one of the architects, "to hear enables one to locate themselves in space outside your own body," and that is precisely what is achieved in the project (Wright 2021).

The project Herbarium, by Eva Susane Oberndorfer, proposes the recovery of an urban ecology by inserting an architecture into an ongoing network of dependencies at the abandoned quarry

Figure 4.7 Ill-defined polycarbonate wall and raised deck allowing the movement of vegetation and water through the building at Baracco+Wright Architects' Garden House, Westernport, Australia.

in Champaner.[3] Prioritizing proximities in order to initiate complex visual and physical connections between inside and outside and between protected and open environments, she imagines the Herbarium as a partially open building. Oberndorfer recreated the line of the original terrain as it might have been before the quarrying began. She inserted the herbarium so that its height and shape took the same form as the section line of the excavation. This was a way to inhabit the vacancy and recall the loss of the land. The building follows the initial form of the terrain to fill it and provide views onto the existing landscape, a visual reminder of the disintegrated site. Furthermore, the Herbarium draws on the existing vegetation on-site and has ramps, openings, and walkways for visitors and researchers to access the plants in their natural habitat—the ruinous site.

In Oberndorfer's design, the exaggerated height of the outer walls creates an enclosed feeling, like being in the mountain. The shape of the building mimics a thick wall, its windows providing views of the outside. A ramp winds from the inside to the outside and back again to the archives. One can walk along it to approach the quarry hill face and the vegetation on it and experience the many plants growing in the courtyard. The public archive faces the big basalt cliff and frames the vegetation growing on it. Visitors become aware of the hybrid conditions of the cliff outside while studying the plant archive inside—small and big windows both separate and connect them to the vegetation—stone hybrid conditions of the site. An open staircase in one corner connects the archive to the office. The office spaces look outside and are often intercepted by gardens enclosed within double-height walls. These gardens provide the experience of having different rooms in one space, ensuring that the staff stay connected to the vegetation. The gardens ensure not only light and fresh air but also a vertical connection to the rooms above.

3 Part of Mithal's spring 2019 undergraduate studio "Terrain-Vague Bricolage: Herbarium in an Abandoned Quarry at Champaner," at CEPT University.

Oberndorfer also studied the microscopic qualities of the rhyolite and basalt stone found in the quarry. Using those properties, she created a rammed-earth composition of load-bearing walls. In each layer a different pigment is added that resembles one of the colors visible only in a microscopic image. To ensure the structural integrity of the high wall, a small amount of cement is added to its composition of soil and gravel. The rammed earth also ensures a comfortable room climate owing to its high thermal mass. **Fig 4.8**

Figure 4.8 Architecture as an insert in an ongoing network of dependencies.

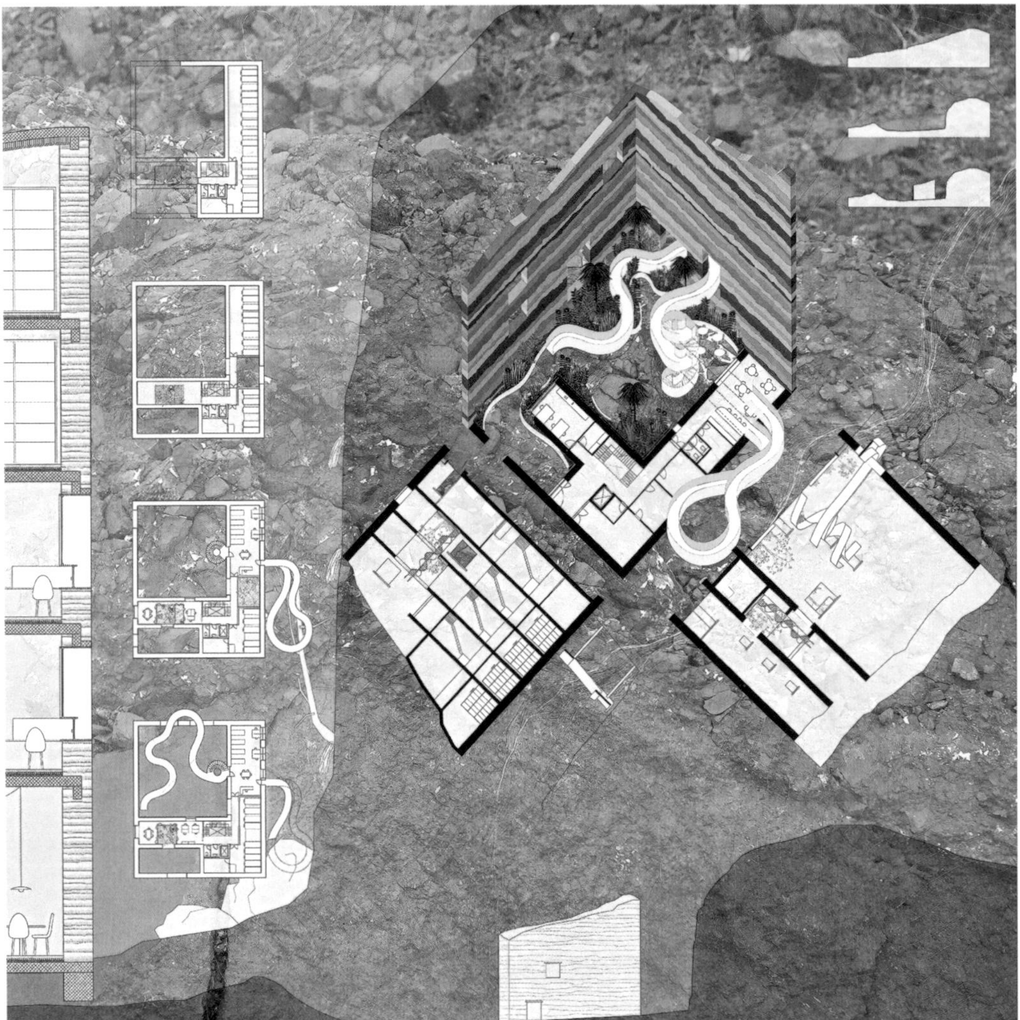

Architecture of Eventual Hybridity

Dusty Relief, a 2002 project by François Roche, Stephanie Lavaux, Jean Navarro, and Pascal Bertholio of the office R&Sie(n), is an example of tentacular thinking in architecture. It uses the potential of a surface's receptivity to catch, embrace, and sustain dust. It is a building enclosed by electromagnetic wires that act as tentacles to receive dust. Antithetical to object-oriented architecture, which prioritizes visual cleanliness, the project removes the structure from visual consumption, shrouding it in a veil of grime. It works with a force of nature instead of resisting it.

Borrowing from Man Ray's *Dust Breeding,* a 1920 photograph of Marcel Duchamp's work *The Large Glass*, which foregrounds dust's materialist tendencies to subvert an artwork, Dusty Relief collects dust. Situated in Bangkok, the project uses an electrostatic mechanism to collect particles of carbon monoxide on an aluminum envelope. A proposal for a contemporary art museum, the project combines the stark Euclidean geometry of interior spaces with the organic topological geometry of a gray ectoplasm. The human habitat is composed of interior cubes and labyrinths, with a controlled climatic environment for museum activities. The nonhuman habitat, on the other hand, is a topological exterior skin composed of electrically charged wires. These wires attract airborne dirt through electrostatic impulses. The project does not resist dust nor does it pretend to remove it or direct it elsewhere. It lets the building get shrouded by a coat of dust. It highlights the issue of pollution by making it visible through its own body, as if carrying the burden on its shoulders. Airborne particulate matter in Bangkok is a result of vehicle emissions, coal combustion, biomass burning, secondary aerosol formation, industrial emissions, sea salt, and other dust sources (Ahmad et al. 2022, 14294). Its constituents make dust a threat to human, plant, and animal life.[4] The project attempts to absorb it, cleaning the environment and making it suitable for habitation.

Dust is a combination of pollen, seeds, soil minerals, fibers, and dead skin. Dusty Relief recalibrates the accumulation of dust as a habitat for microorganisms. The project also makes visible the labor involved in removing dust. The building's use of technology to absorb the particles subverts the labor required to clean and maintain built environments. It upends oppressive practices that employ manual labor to keep the surfaces of buildings clean. Fig 4.9 The conservation architect Jorge Otero-

4 The particulate matter comprises carbonaceous components such as elemental carbon and organic carbon as well as water-soluble inorganic species resulting from meteorological and geographical conditions, industrial particle emissions, transportation, and agriculture (Ahmad et al. 2022, 14282). Aerosol in Bangkok contains iron, calcium, aluminum, arsenic, lead, vanadium, and barium (Matthews et al. 2022, 79040).

Figure 4.9 Electrostatic mesh laid on the building and the section showing accumulated dust on the building of Dusty Relief, Bangkok.

Pailos calls for a similar need to eradicate practices of manual labor for cleaning facades. When settled on the surface, dust is less hazardous to the structure than it is to the workers cleaning it. He questions the modernist insistence on seeing the dust stains on architecture as pollution (Otero-Pailos 2010, 132). In his exhibition project *The Ethics of Dust* (2009), he cleaned a wall of the Doge's Palace in Venice that was never seen by tourists and hence never cleaned. He used a liquid latex, which, on drying, removed the dust in its original configuration on the wall's stone surface, revealing how dust, excluded in modernism as a cultural symbol of pollution, embodies the fundamental instability of the architectural object. The project comments on the necessity of integrating pollution into architecture, its history, and its preservation.

The project To Bee, proposed by Aswin Senthil at the abandoned quarry in Champaner, employs the skin of the building as an ecological agent—an ecotone.[5] Imagined as a center for apiculture and horticulture, it creates a human habitat while initiating a condition for the nonhuman—bees and plants—to assume agency as the human built environment slowly deteriorates. It focuses on making the building facade bioreceptive as well as mutable. Drawing on similar research undertaken at the Delft University of Technology (Lubelli et al. 2021), the project identified key design principles. First, the moisture transport of the brick-mortar combination is crucial for bioreceptivity.[6] Instead of wire-cut or extruded bricks, bricks sized 210 × 100 × 50 mm were molded from soft mud and contained a frog, or cavity, to help retain water and soil within the wall construction, further favoring bioreceptivity. To Bee imagines a facade constructed of brick and mortar made of natural hydraulic lime, cement, and sand. The addition of vermiculite—a lightweight aggregate—to the mortar was proposed for its proven benefits for plant growth. Vermiculite is highly porous, which makes it work as a water reservoir. It also contains a high ion exchange capacity, which provides a buffer for the supply of nutrients to plants.[7]

Following observations from Pickers Mill—that plant growth generally occurs in mortar joints—and studying the path that tree roots have taken through cavities, To Bee proposes a specific brick pattern. The pattern envisages mortar joints of varying thickness placed in a row to ensure that the tree roots can find their way without any obstacle and simultaneously strengthen their connection with the wall. A specific mortar and brick type that can ensure moisture retention as well as movement needs to be used. Fig 4.10

To Bee proposes adding seeds of phototropic native plants such as climbing fig to the mortar. Wind-borne seeds might also get sedimented on exposed mortar joints.[8] The project uses plaster with bigger aggregates, mortar of varying thickness, and gabion walls to allow and direct plants to grow on the facade. Plants occupy the bioreceptive surface of the structure; propagated through bees, they constantly morph the structure. As the project slowly mutates over time, just the outer skin remains as an assemblage available to be taken over by new life-forms. The organic

5 Senthil's project is part of Mithal's studio "Ecotone—The Sentient Ruins: Ecological Recovery at an Abandoned Quarry, Champaner, India," offered at CEPT University in spring 2021.

6 These bricks have shown a far greater favorability for plant growth, working as a water reservoir for the mortar. Mortar's very fine pores allow it to extract water from the brick by capillarity and retain it long enough for the plants to grow (Lubelli et al. 2020, 11). Lubelli et al.'s research has revealed that mortars made of natural hydraulic lime, cement, and sand are best for bedding mortar, while hydraulic lime and trass mortar is best for pointing.

Figure 4.10
Bioreceptive walls.

thrives as the inorganic construction system slowly recedes in a controlled manner. The renewal of a disturbed site is proposed through ruination itself. It imagines Haraway's terrapolis, a recuperating terra's pluriverse, existing across time. Hiving requires direct access, protection from sunlight, an ambient temperature of 28–35 degrees Celsius, and the presence of pollen. Old hives when overpopulated lead to the creation of new ones. Similar to plants, grafting helps to accelerate the formation of bees' natural habitat. To Bee is situated in the ruins in such a manner that the conditions of a beehive are met on its outer skin. It accommodates a response to the spatiality of the ruin and a response to aesthetics. Plant invasion on the facade triggers a condition that accelerates the bee population. The apiculture lab runs as long as the ruination process has not been initiated. When that happens, the building slowly becomes less habitable for humans and more habitable for bees and vegetation. The skin of the building, on becoming a multispecies habitat, acts as a veil for the architecture. Bees and vegetation overtaking the facade contributes to a controlled ruination of the structure. As bees and plants take over, architecture becomes reappropriated, adapts, and becomes receptive to its dissolution and changed function over time. "Proposed actions are germinal. A start is defined, but its evolution is simulated through one of the many probabilities. Time is a design tool. The design act here is simply a catalyst to a long and uncertain process" (Senthil 2021).

The project Productive Erosions, proposed by Lukas Ryffel for Pickers Mill in Ahmedabad, aims to recover an urban ecology by putting the ruinous condition of an abandoned factory to use by channeling waste into hybrid systems.[9] Vegetation and animals, including humans, are encouraged to use the ruin as a site for growth. The informal occupiers of the Pickers Mill—erstwhile factory workers, vegetation, monkeys, birds, debris—are constantly stabilizing the effects of a destabilized environment. This balance is self-induced and does not follow a systematic logic or project any classification-based dichotomies regarding humans, machines, waste, or ruins. The ecology of the ruinous site—manifested in vegetation growing out of broken walls, corroding steel, or people finding ways to persevere—demands a rede-

7 In the previous experiment, mortars to which plant seeds were added during mixing were the most successful (Lubelli et al. 2020, 9). Seeds of ivy-leafed toadflax (Cymbalaria muralis) and yellow corydalis (Pseudofumaria lutea) were added to mortars. Ivy-leafed toadflax has an unusual method of propagation. Initially, the flower stalk is positively phototropic and moves toward the light. After fertilization, it becomes negatively phototropic ("scototropic") and moves away from the light. This results in seeds being pushed into dark crevices of rock walls, where they are more likely to germinate. Yellow corydalis requires light shade with good moisture, but will tolerate both full sun and deep shade. It grows in cracks in old walls where drainage is excellent.

8 Lubelli et al.'s prototypes also attracted wind-borne seeds, confirming that the mortar mix has the capacity to germinate seeds brought by wind to the exposed mortar joints.

9 Part of Mithal's undergraduate architecture studio "Terrain-Vague Bricolage: Reterritorializing Urban Ruins of Abandoned Mills in Ahmedabad," offered by CEPT University, Ahmedabad, in spring 2018.

finition of revitalization that incorporates a hint of life into the otherwise derelict place. In this understanding, the site is *elemental* and hence offers an ideal condition for the experiment. The process of ruination is a collaborative act by various forces on a structure, dissolving the designed form more and more. The space acquires a new aesthetic and new possibilities of use. A new space develops that is not clear in its usage and whose function is not dominated by anyone but is productive for the different actors involved.

Ryffel mapped the relationship of the ruin and the banyan tree (*Ficus benghalensis*) and identified places that were invaded and endangered by aerial roots and seeds. These readings were assessed for potential design interventions. At the places where aerial roots were strangling the structure, cracking the roof, and disrupting the structural integrity of the wall, a steel structural member was incorporated to stabilize the tree's growth over time. The original building might degrade and a new structure emerge as an outcome of the collaboration between brick, steel, and vegetation. This might also make the tree grow in a new manner. The growth of aerial roots could be steered to make space for additional rooms. Ryffel further mapped the relationship of the banyan tree and the ruin and identified places that were endangered by seed invasion and high humidity. Here, new walls were envisaged that trees can grow alongside, providing a shaded canopy and green wall. **Fig 4.11** A temporary pond was formed and an existing water tank was cleaned up and put into use, irrigating the site through pipes along the walls. **Fig 4.12**

To facilitate this productive erosion, an irrigation machine was introduced. This machine, similar to the trees, is a parasite on the host of the built structure, and distributes water and nutrients to increase urban agriculture in this dry zone of India. A tension is created between the ruin and the machine. The machine is dependent on the ruin but at the same time promotes its destruction; hence, the machine is endangering itself. Trees grow along the walls using the water provided by the machine, slowly replacing them. An intertwined condition develops where ruin, machine, vegetation, and animals start to become one. The machine is designed to promote growth on the site. Structurally, it uses elements of the ruin in a similar way to the banyan tree, stabilizing certain parts, endangering others. It is sometimes parasitic, sometimes symbiotic. But through its close relationship with the ruin and its function—promoting plant growth—it endangers itself. **Fig 4.13**

Figure 4.11 Potential design interventions following a mapping of places endangered by aerial root invasion and seed invasion.

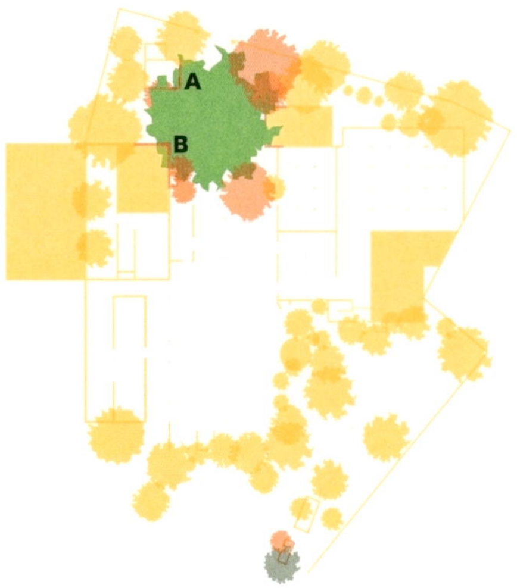

- Ficus Benghalensis
- Invaded by aerial roots
- Endangered by aerial root invasion
- Endangered by seed invasion

- Ficus Religiosa
- Invaded structures
- Endangered due to higher humidity
- Endangered by seed invasion

Design Possibilities at A **Design Possibilities at B** **Design Possibilities at C**

Figure 4.12 Axonometric view of Productive Erosions.

Figure 4.13 Visuals of Productive Erosions.

Architecture of Prosthetics

Treasure Hill by Marco Casagrande situates itself in an existing network of dependencies at a postindustrial ruin as an organic machine. In 2003, Casagrande was commissioned to make an ecological master plan for Treasure Hill in Taipei, an urban squatter settlement on the Guanyin hillside southwest of the Taiwanese capital. During the Second World War, Treasure Hill served as an anti-aircraft position for the Japanese army, after which it was taken over by soldiers from the Chinese Nationalist Party. Over time, this military base grew into a settlement as the soldiers and their families built homes in, and atop, the bunkers. Having lost its strategic value,

Treasure Hill was transformed from a military base into an unofficial settlement of soldiers' families—a slum. City officials wanted to demolish the ruinous squatter settlement and introduce a park instead. Yet, Casagrande saw the ruination of Treasure Hill as favorable to creating an urban area that allows various species and elements to cohabit. "Ruin is when man-made has become part of nature" (Casagrande 2014). He argues that it is through ruination that an industrial city becomes an organic city.

Officially recognized as an illegal settlement, Treasure Hill is secluded from the surrounding city. This condition gave rise to various self-organized systems of rainwater collection and gray-water filtering. A system of urban gardening was established through cultivation in passive solar houses on the hillside and compost using the waste of the settlement and the surrounding city. Treasure Hill is tentacular and self-made; it leaches onto the official city, siphoning off water and electricity. Casagrande realized that the residents had implemented an intuitive ecological model precisely because of the settlement's illegal and marginalized status. Treasure Hill permeates the adjacent forest and allows wildlife to permeate the settlement. Plants grow from the cracks in the plinths and walls of the houses and take over the surfaces. This vegetation growth goes against the norms of human control. Casagrande reads these ad-hoc systems and fragmented community gardens within Treasure Hill as the "acupuncture needles" needed to propel the collective underlying organic energy of the industrial city and translate the mechanical city into an organic one (Casagrande 2014).

Going beyond the master plan, Casagrande protested the demolition, instead proposing minimal interventions such as platforms, bamboo bridges, and spaces for the farmers market. He constructed wooden stairways and walkway connections between the dilapidated houses and shelters for the older residents to play mahjong and ping-pong. He strengthened the existing "urban ecology laboratory" informally initiated and maintained by the residents (Casagrande 2014). We read this as an assemblage with its own conduits for matter and energy flows, a network of post-industrial urban memories, and a robust, resilient ecological system. His intervention inserts itself as a

Figure 4.14 Minimal architectural interventions at Treasure Hill in Taipei, Taiwan.

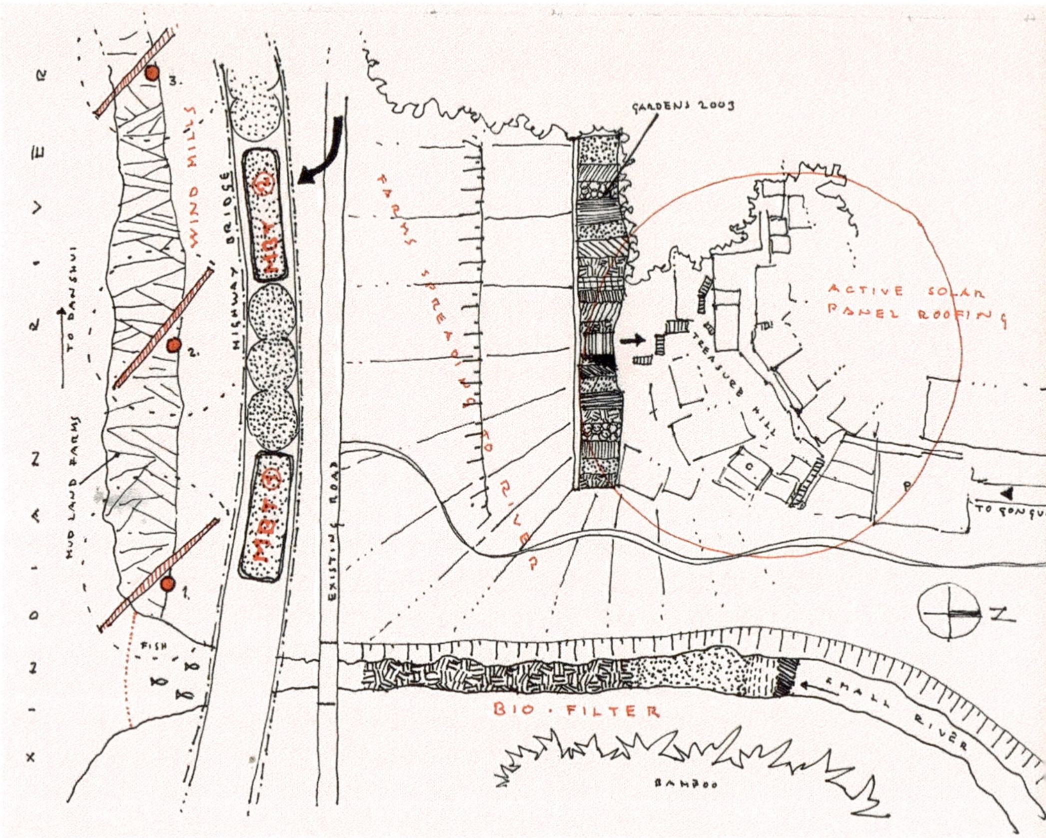

10 **Wadhwa's project is part of Mithal's studio "Ecotone—The Sentient Ruins: Ecological Recovery at an Abandoned Quarry, Champaner, India," offered at CEPT University in spring 2021.**

prosthetic into an existing assemblage to strengthen it and further consolidate the ongoing networks. **Fig 4.14, Fig 4.15**
The project Ethno-Botanical Institute, proposed by Aastha Wadhwa at the abandoned quarry in Champaner, triggers a recovery of the distressed landscape by accelerating the ongoing processes of renewal.[10] Architecture is positioned as a material-tectonic-environmental interface between ecological and infrastructural requirements. Wadhwa identifies locations where surface-water runoff naturally accumulated as potential zones for secondary reservoirs. The reservoirs store the excess water collected during monsoons, ensuring a continuous supply of water for the drier periods. This water is used in the service areas of the Ethno-Botanical Institute and to maintain the proposed botanical garden. Excess water from the secondary reservoirs is transported to the primary reservoir (the existing body of water) through bioswales. Watershed simulations are generated on Grasshopper to calculate the capacity of each reservoir, with the assumption that only 60 percent of the water will success-

fully reach the reservoir, the remaining 40 percent being lost either through cracks or evaporation. The institute is placed in an empty space where there was previously a pile of debris. To ensure accessibility, one of the pre-existing paths formed by human movement is retained, providing a route to and from the structure.

Sentient mappings revealed that erosion has led to deposits of soil in the crevices and fractures of the basalt rock. The uneven surface of the rock made it receptive to debris and subsequently it could support vegetation growth, the roots of which stabilize the weakened rock. An ongoing process of renewal is embedded in the process of ruination. Wadhwa speculates about how to emulate these conditions to bring the ecological mechanisms into architectural thinking. Her intervention prioritizes response-ability. Tapping into the opportunity created by the uneven rock surfaces, she uses a mesh made from bioreceptive concrete.[11] The mesh serves as a response to hydrological forces, amplifying the water channels and directing runoff to the secondary reservoir, and as a response to plant life, allowing soil to settle in and encouraging perennial vegetation growth as opposed to the current seasonal cycle, thus accelerating the natural process. The mesh is anchored at certain locations so that it does not disrupt the ecosystems already present on the cliff. Basalt is impervious in nature and hence allows water to traverse its surface.

11 Wadhwa adapts the works of Marcos Cruz and Nina Jotanovic for this purpose. Cruz has studied the biologically receptive cementitious materials and chemically altered them to provide pH levels, porosity values, and water-retention properties that are favorable for microorganisms to establish and proliferate. Jotanovic uses microbial colonization, biomineralization, and the self-assembly of nano-scale building blocks to produce biological micro-crusts in ecologically benign processes.

Slope, gravity, water velocity, and surface area were factored into designing the morphology of the mesh. On a gentle slope, the water travels at a slower velocity and requires a larger surface area—hence, the width of the channel is wider on top. As the slope becomes steeper, the velocity of the water increases, and the same amount of water requires less surface area (velocity of water being inversely proportional to the surface area required)—hence, the width of the channel is reduced at the bottom. The niches, too, respond to these factors. Where there is a gentle slope, the soil can settle in a slight protrusion, and where the slope is steep, a larger protrusion is necessary. The mesh is affixed to the basalt rock with stainless steel clamps and anchor bolts. Over time, the mesh is ex-

Figure 4.15 Vegetal growth over buildings at Treasure Hill in Taipei, Taiwan.

pected to be taken over by microorganisms, obscuring the architectural intervention.

The morphology of the outer envelope responds to the existing hydrological forces, directing surface runoff into the reservoir, and thus acting as a prosthetic. A water channel over this envelope directs the flow of water. Along with the bioreceptive outer envelope, the bioreceptive mesh is proposed as a permanent intervention, whereas the inner structure can be dismantled and stands independent of the outer shell. It is expected to become a homogenous part of the site, responding to ecological forces even after the inner structure has been taken away. The envelope serves as an ecotone as it negotiates between the ecological and infrastructural requirements.

The surface geometry of the undulating pattern on the surface of the bioreceptive envelope has been designed in such a way that it slows down the movement of water, provides a cushion for microbial habitats, and creates shade and a wind buffer. Additionally, the surface consists of microgrooves, which help to retain moisture and provide a rough surface where algae can anchor. This geometry mimics the existing conditions of the uneven basalt rock surface that facilitate microbial growth on-site.

The envelope consists of roughly three layers. The top environmentally active layer is made of bioreceptive concrete, the middle protective layer for waterproofing is made of silicon, and the bottom structural layer is constructed using ferro-cement. Basalt fiber is added to the ferro-cement mix, which improves its flexural strength to support the weight of water flowing along the top layer. Algae is expected to first grow along the edges, leaving space for the continuous movement of water. The proposed intervention would mutate over time to facilitate multispecies habitation. It also aims to obscure itself, acting as an infrastructure for water retention, plant growth, organic inhabitation, and the overall recovery of the distressed landscape.

The site is imagined as a body and the proposed intervention a prosthetic that allows the site to recover by responding to and accelerating the natural processes of renewal. The intervention further adapts to the changing conditions once it has surpassed the requirement for human needs, thus going beyond the idea of serving only as a prosthetic. Fig 4.16

The project Basalt Building Material Research Laboratory, proposed by Nehal Jain at the abandoned quarry in Champaner, is imagined as an architecture of prosthetics.[12] Jain reads the landscape of the quarry as a system of vacancies created during the blasting process. The vacancies in the harder basalt cliff face were created from the drilling and blasting, whereas the voids in the softer mud terrain are attributed to continuous foot traffic and

12 Jain's project is part of Mithal's studio "Ecotone—The Sentient Ruins: Ecological Recovery at an Abandoned Quarry, Champaner, India," offered at CEPT University in spring 2021.

Figure 4.16 Architecture to accelerate renewal of a ruin.

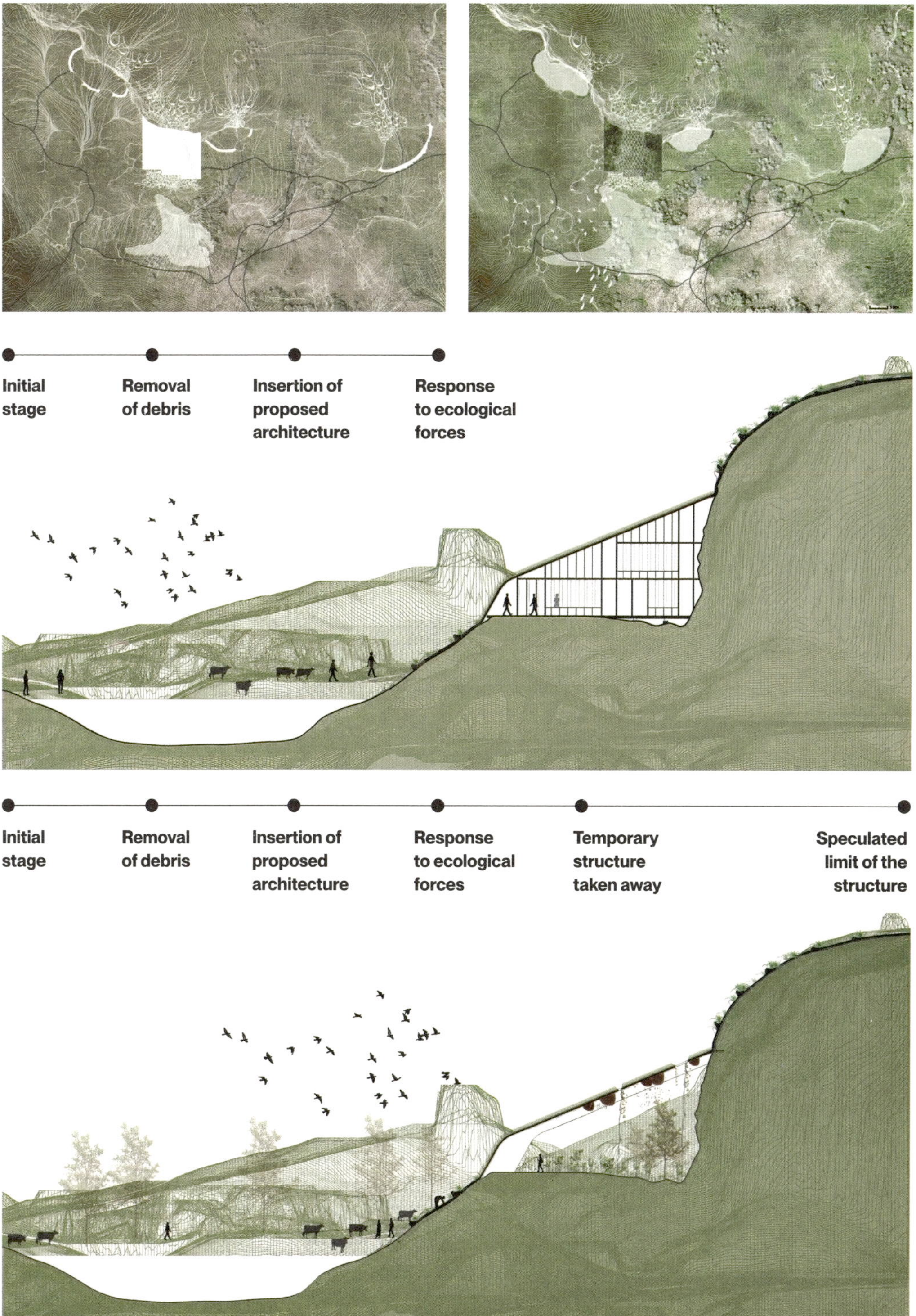

water runoff. These vacancies become potential spaces in which to attach new architectural forms as prosthetics. Jain identifies two types of vacancies—those that consist of a terrace-like horizontal surface on the quarry face itself and those cave-like cavities adjacent to the terraces. Diverse in size, these vacancies are located at different heights in the quarry. Most of them are interconnected via ledge-like vacancies, narrow strips that project from the cliff face. The ledges are often characterized by the presence of vegetation. When seen from a distance, horizontal strips of vegetation on the hill face indicate their location. Eroding clay has collected at these places and become microhabitats for various plant species.

Jain identified two conditions conducive to her prosthetic intervention—maximum surface runoff and a wide horizontal plane on the hill abutting a tall vertical plane. Her primary strategy was to link the wide horizontal planes via ledges at various levels, freeing up space on the ground for the vegetal, geological, hydrological, and animal to continue with their habitations. The built form is raised above ground and has a very light mass above. Over time, different hybrid conditions develop. The skin of the building acts as an ecological agent and an interface for multispecies interrelationships to flourish.

Jain treats design not only as a way to link fractured rocks, water bodies, and vegetation as landscape resources, but also to shape space, restore vegetation, and create viewpoints. With an emphasis on celebrating the site, the intervention, guided by the visual spectacularity of the ruin, converts the quarry into a cultural space with areas of experimentation. The architecture is designed to eventually disappear into the landscape of the existing quarry. The structure is visible even though it blends with its surroundings. The project uses basalt blocks obtained from the site. Interventions create and connect new functional spaces that can be used as laboratories and ancillary services for the scientific research of basalt fiber manufacture. Hiking routes will be converted into new pedestrian paths to access the quarry site.

Envisaged as a light structure, the building is constructed with metal, basalt fiber, and rammed earth. It is integrated with the quarry surface, where the more-than-human thrives, collecting water, stopping erosion, and strengthening crevices to propel the place into an accelerated state of multispecies collaboration. The rammed-earth walls are positioned separately from the hill face, creating a protected environment in which various species can thrive. The floor plan consists of a laboratory space and a research center. A courtyard at the back extends to the cliff face—a transitional space that serves as an ecotone between the organic and the inorganic. Multiple terraces have been integrated architecturally to forget connections with the cliff surface and the overall site. The intention behind the project is to build something that allows the site to renew itself over time. The rammed-earth walls are expected to last and the light metal structure can be completely removed in the future. Thus, the building acts as a prosthetic that accelerates and strengthens the ecology of the place while it is there, serving a human purpose on the side. Once the ecological recovery has been initiated, it can be removed. **Fig 4.17, Fig 4.18**

Figure 4.17 Prosthetic intervention elevation.

Figure 4.18 Prosthetic intervention section.

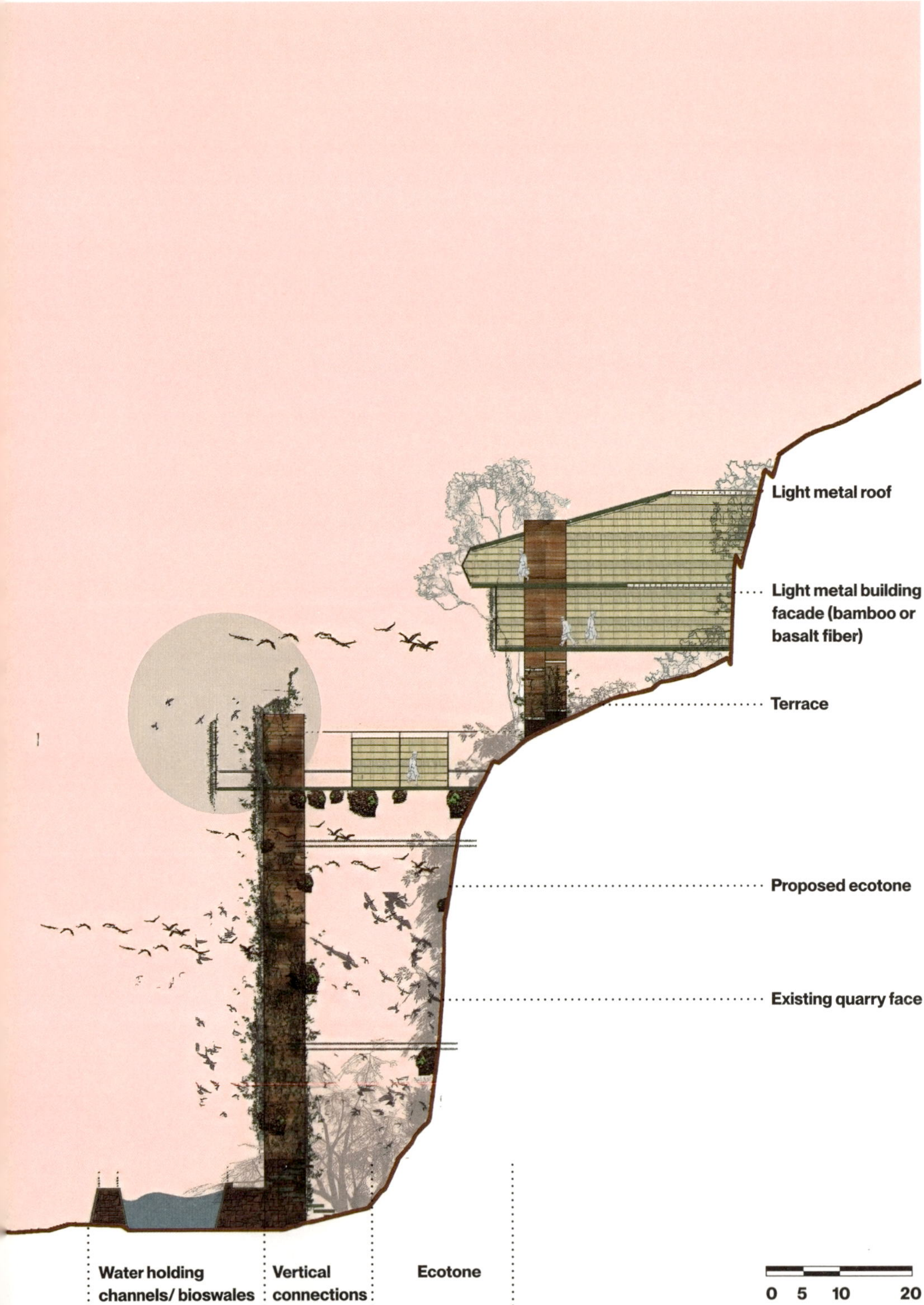

Conclusion

In *Living Together*, we discuss the antithetical relationship between modern architecture and more-than-human species. Recognizing modern architecture's role in the ongoing emergency of species loss, we optimistically invite architects to recalibrate their role in partially recuperating the damaged ecosystems. Ascertaining a need to holistically consider multispecies habitat in architectural design, we demonstrate how the processes of ruination reveal multispecies entanglements, resulting from viewing the characteristics of ruins as opportunities. We see fractures and fissures as opportunities, whereby conventional architecture deems them unworthy or undesirable. By centering these characteristics, we show that, in order for architecture to host multispecies relationships, it must go beyond its modernist ideals of longevity, permanence, determinacy, cleanliness, and sterility.

This book demonstrates that an anticipated recovery of broken ecological cycles does not require big architectural actions. Rather, an architectural response may limit itself to activating or setting conditions conducive to multispecies habitats. These conditions are essentially those seen in ruins. The ruin's vulnerability becomes the precise reason for sheltering multiple life-forms. The ruin in its materiality is sentient with the agency to adapt to the changing environment, and hence survive. Decay in organic matter, the coexistence of igneous and sedimentary rocks, and the presence of emerging vegetation in cracks shows that the various actors in ruins are response-able.

Mapping Sentience helps architecture acknowledge the ways a ruin rejuvenates itself. It helps to identify where conditions of ruination and fracture have adapted themselves to become conditions for renewal and stabilization. Sentience is mapped through evidence of hybridity to identify how seemingly incongruent materials start to form a symbiotic existence, through found evidence of ruination and renewal to identify how decay has the potential to regenerate itself and its surroundings, through found evidence of vacancies to identify the factors whose absence led to landscape distress, and through found spatial systems formed by broken basalt to identify how space—in terms of surfaces and edges—gets created when a stone breaks along a line of structural weakness. Mapping these processes systematically indicates design elements that could drive architectural interventions.

Mapping waste, abandonment, and materiality at ruins makes a case for envisaging architecture as an ecotone generated from possibilities offered by redundancy. In this understanding, ruination and vulnerability can lead to hybrid materials that have the potential to make architecture adaptable and hence sustainable.

This book develops a vocabulary suitable for architectural thinking and practice that enables architects to evaluate the potential of their sites for multispecies habitats. Architecture needs to respond to indicators of sentience, such as hybridity, vacancy, disintegration, water, wind, gravity, and erosion. The ecological actors dwell in the ruins as if in an assemblage. An assemblage has a materiality, form, and tectonics. Understanding assemblages equips architecture to formulate a response strategy. We develop a new framework for reading sites as more-than-human assemblages, translating the characteristics of assemblages into an architectural act with a spatial, material, and formal component. Treating all architecture as assemblages, this book proposes that an architectural act can perform *tentacularity*, acknowledge *vacancy*, embrace *hybridity*, act as a *prosthetic*, be composed of *receptive* surfaces, and embody an *indeterminate* form.

The interconnectedness of life on earth means that humans are an inextricable part of more-than-human ecologies and systems. Humans building their homes and workplaces must do so alongside more-than-human species building their homes and workplaces. Human architecture thus becomes part of an interconnected habitat. The collective knowledge of multiple species, including humans, makes for resilient environments premised on collaborations and forging kinship. Reworking our architectural agendas now can ensure that the future is better when we are living together.

A

AABR (Australian Association of Bush Regenerators). 2013. "The Bradley Method." AABR Working with Natural Processes, April 11. ↗ https://www.aabr.org.au/learn/what-i-bush-regeneration/general-principles/the-bradley-method/.

AHMAD, Mushtaq, Thanaphum MANJANTRARAT, Wachiraya RATTANAWONGSA, Phitchaya MUENSRI, Rattaporn SAENMUANGCHIN, Annop KLAMCHUEN, Sasitorn AUEVIRIYAVIT, Kanokwan SUKRAK, Wiyong KANGWANSUPAMONKON, and Sirima PANYAMETHEEKUL. 2022. "Chemical Composition, Sources, and Health Risk Assessment of PM2.5 and PM10 in Urban Sites of Bangkok, Thailand." *International Journal of Environmental Research and Public Health* 19 (21): 14281. ↗ https://doi.org/10.3390/ijerph192114281.

AHMED, Sara. 2006. *Queer Phenomenology: Orientations, Objects, Others*. Duke University Press.

AMIRKHANI, Aryan, Hanie OKHOVAT, and Ehsan ZAMANI. 2010. "Ancient Pigeon Houses: Remarkable Example of the Asian Culture Crystallized in the Architecture of Iran and Central Anatolia." *Asian Culture and History* 2 (2): 45–57.

ANKLESARIA, Sarosh. 2021. "Cooking New Worlds: From Machinic Architectures to Biome Ecologies." *Strelka Mag*. ↗ https://strelkamag.com/en/article/urban-symbiome. Accessed on September 15, 2022.

B

BALES, Rebecca. 2024. "Funambulus Palmarum." *AZ Animals*. ↗ https://a-z-animals.com/animals/indian-palm-squirrel/ Accessed on June 27, 2024

Baroda Heritage Trust and People for Heritage Concern. 2004a. "Champaner-Pavagadh Archaeological Park Maps." UNESCO. ↗ https://whc.unesco.org/en/list/1101/multiple=1&unique_number=1279. Accessed on December 14, 2021.

Baroda Heritage Trust and People for Heritage Concern. 2004b. "World Heritage Nomination Champaner-Pavagadh Archaeological Park Documents." UNESCO. Accessed on December 14, 2021. ↗ https://whc.unesco.org/en/list/1101/documents/

BAUMANN, Céline, and Ethel Baraona POHL. 2020. "The Parliament of Plants and Other Cautionary Tales, Where Stories Make Worlds and Worlds Make Stories." *Solitude Journal 1: Collective Care & Response-ability*: 72–81.

BIRCH, Amanda. 2016. "Reinventing the Green Wall." *Building Design Magazine*, April 15. ↗ https://www.bdonline.co.uk/buildings/reinventing-the-green-wall/5081204.article. Accessed on January 4, 2023.

BENNETT, Jane. 2010. *Vibrant Matter: A Political Ecology of Things*. Duke University Press.

BOETZKES, Amanda. 2010. *The Ethics of Earth Art.* University of Minnesota Press.

C

CARROLL, Lewis. 1895. *Sylvie and Bruno Concluded.* Macmillan and Co.

CARSTEN, Janet. 2003. *After Kinship.* Cambridge University Press.

CASAGRANDE, Marco. 2008. "Cross-Over Architecture and the Third Generation City." *Epifanio* 9. ↗ http://www.epifanio.eu/nr9/eng/cross-over.html.

CASAGRANDE, Marco. 2014. "Paracity: Urban Acupuncture." *Public Spaces Bratislava*, November 20.

CASEY, Edward. 2005. *Earth-Mapping: Artists Reshaping Landscape*. University of Minnesota Press.

CEBALLOS, Gerardo, Paul R. EHRLICH, Anthony D. BARNOSKY, Andrés GARCÍA, Robert M. PRINGLE, and Todd M. PALMER. 2015. "Accelerated Modern Human-Induced Species Losses: Entering the Sixth Mass Extinction." *Science Advances* 1 (5). ↗ https://doi.org/10.1126/sciadv.1400253.

CHAVAN, Appasaheb Ramachandrarao, and Gunvantrai Maneklal OZA. 1966. *The Flora of Pavagadh, Gujarat State*. Department of Botany, Maharaja Sayajirao University. ↗ http://hdl.handle.net/10603/59863.

CLARK, Timothy. 2015. *Ecocriticism on the Edge: The Anthropocene as a Threshold Concept*. Bloomsbury Academic.

CLÉMENT, Gilles. 2015. *"The Planetary Garden" and Other Writings*. Translated by Sandra Morris. University of Pennsylvania Press.

COLOMINA, Beatriz. 2019. *X-Ray Architecture.* Lars Müller Publishers.

CORNER, James. 1999. "The Agency of Mapping Speculation, Critique and Invention." In *Mappings*, edited by Denis Cosgrove. Reaktion.

CRUZ, Marcos. 2022. *Poikilohydric Living Walls*. Bartlett Design Research Folios.

D

DELANDA, Manuel. 1997. *A Thousand Years of Nonlinear History*. MIT Press.

DELANDA, Manuel. 2006. *A New Philosophy of Society: Assemblage Theory and Social Complexity*. Continuum.

DELEUZE, Gilles, and Félix GUATTARI. 1985. *A Thousand Plateaus: Capitalism and Schizophrenia.* University of Minnesota Press.

DESPRET, Vinciane. 2017. "Afterword: It Is an Entire World That Has Disappeared." In *Extinction Studies: Stories of Time, Death, and Generations*, edited by Deborah Bird Rose, Thom van Doorne, and Matthew Chrulew. Columbia University Press.

DOUGLAS, Mary. 1966. *Purity and Danger: An Analysis of Concepts of Pollution and Taboo*. Routledge.

E

EDENSOR, Tim. 2005. *Industrial Ruins: Space, Aesthetics and Materiality*. Bloomsbury Academic.

ELBERT, Wolfgang, Bettina WEBER, Susannah BURROWS, Jörg STEINKAMP; Burkhard BÜDEL, Meinrat O. ANDREAE, and Ulrich PÖSCHL. 2012. "Contribution of Cryptogamic Covers to the Global Cycles of Carbon and Nitrogen." *Nature Geoscience* 5 (7): 459–62. ↗ https://doi.org/10.1038/ngeo1486.

ELHACHAM, Emily, Liad BEN-URI, Jonathan GROZOVSKI, Yinon M. BAR-ON, and Ron Milo. 2020. "Global Human-Made Mass Exceeds All Living Biomass." *Nature* 588: 442–44. ↗ https://doi.org/10.1038/s41586-020-3010-5.

ESCOBAR, Arturo. 1999. "After Nature: Steps to an Antiessentialist Political Ecology." *Current Anthropology* 40 (1): 1–30. ↗ https://doi.org/10.1086/515799.

F

FISHEL, Stefanie R. 2017. *The Microbial State: Global Thriving and the Body Politic*. University of Minnesota Press.

FLEMING, Theodore H., Cullen GEISELMAN, and Walter John KRESS. 2009. "The Evolution of Bat Pollination: A Phylogenetic Perspective." *Annals of Botany* 104 (6): 1017–43. ↗ https://doi.org/10.1093/aob/mcp197.

FLORY, Ashley. 2019. "Psittacula krameria." *Animal Diversity Web*. ↗ https://animaldiversity.org/accounts/Psittacula_krameri/ Accessed on March 22, 2023.

FRANK, Eyal, and Anant SUDARSHAN. 2023. "The Social Costs of Keystone Species Collapse: Evidence from the Decline of Vultures in India." University of Chicago, Becker Friedman Institute for Economics Working Paper No. 2022-165. ↗ https://doi.org/10.2139/ssrn.4318579.

FRICHOT, Hélène. 2019. *Dirty Theory: Troubling Architecture*. Spurbuchverlag Baunach.

FRICHOT, Hélène. 2023. "Dirty Materialism: What Jennifer Knew." *The Journal of Architecture* 28 (6): 996–1021.

FRICHOT, Hélène, and Stephen LOO. 2013. *Deleuze and Architecture*. Edinburgh University Press.

G

GAJJAR, Akshar. 2021. *Adapting Multispecies Studies in Architectural Thinking.* Unpublished bachelor's thesis. Faculty of Architecture, CEPT University. ↗ http://hdl.handle.net/20.500.12725/26536

GATTO, Gionata, and John R. McCARDLE. 2019. "Multispecies Design and Ethnographic Practice: Following Other-than-Humans as a Mode of Exploring Environmental Issues." *Sustainability* 11 (18): 5032. ↗ https://doi.org/10.3390/su11185032.

GINSBERG, Robert. 2004. *The Aesthetic of Ruins*. Rodopi BV.

GISSEN, David. 2009. *Subnature: Architecture's Other Environments*. Princeton Architectural Press.

GLAIZE, Maurice, and Jean BOISSELIER. 1993 (1944). *The Monuments of the Angkor Group*. Translation from the fourth French edition. Accessed on March 7, 2023.

GROSS, Matthias. 2010. *Ignorance and Surprise: Science, Society, and Ecological Design*. MIT Press.

GUY, Simon. 2012. "Pragmatic Ecologies." In *Architectural Theories of the Environment: Posthuman Territory*, edited by Ariane Lourie Harrison. Routledge.

H

HARAWAY, Donna J. 1991. *Simians, Cyborgs, and Women: The Reinvention of Nature*. Routledge.

HARAWAY, Donna J. 2003. *The Companion Species Manifesto: Dogs, People, and Significant Otherness*. Chicago University Press.

HARAWAY, Donna J. 2016a. *Manifestly Haraway*. University of Minnesota Press.

HARAWAY, Donna J. 2016b. *Staying with the Trouble: Making Kin in the Chthulucene*. Duke University Press.

HARRISON, Ariane Lourie, ed. 2013. *Architectural Theories of the Environment: Posthuman Territory*. Routledge.

HARRISON, Ariane Lourie. 2017. "'Posthuman' Architecture." *Stream 04 The Paradoxes of Living*. ↗ https://www.pca-stream.com/en/explore/posthuman-architecture-2/.

HUME, Julian P. 2006. "The History of the Dodo Raphus Cucullatus and the Penguin of Mauritius." *Historical Biology* 18 (2): 65–89. ↗ https://doi.org/10.1080/08912960600639400.

I

IUCN. 2024. *The IUCN Red List of Threatened Species*. ↗ https://www.iucnredlist.org/statistics. Accessed on December 27, 2024.

J

JAIN, Anab, and Jon ARDEN. 2021. "Superflux: Refuge for Resurgence." ↗ https://www.labiennale.org/en/architecture/2021/new-households/superflux. La Biennale di Venezia. Accessed on October 3, 2023.

JOSHI, Aditya U. 2019. "Fold Interference Patterns in Meso-Proterozoic Champaner Fold Belt (CFB) Gujarat, Western India." *Journal of Earth System Science* 128 (48). https://doi.org/10.1007/s12040-019-1075-z.

K

KATARA, Botsa. 2021. *The Prosthetic Body: Disabled, Posthuman, a Cyborg, or Still Human?* Doctoral thesis, Durham University.

KHALIFA, Shaden A. M., Esraa H. ELSHAFIEY, Aya A. SHETAIA, Aida A. ABD EL-WAHED, Ahmed F. ALGETHAMI, Syed G. MUSHARRAF, Mohamed F. ALAJMI, et al. 2021. "Overview of Bee Pollination and Its Economic Value for Crop Production." *Insects* 12 (8): 688–711. ↗ https://doi.org/10.3390/insects12080688.

KOTHARI, Ashish, Ariel SALLEH, Arturo ESCOBAR, Federico DE MARIA, Alberto ACOSTA, eds. 2019. *Pluriverse: A Post-Development Dictionary*. Tulika Books.

KOTTEKKATTU, Thoiba, and A. K. PRADEEP. 2020. "A Revision of Tripogon (Poaceae: Chloridoideae) in India." *RHEEDEA Journal of the Indian Association for Angiosperm Taxonomy* 30 (3): 325–78. ↗ https://dx.doi.org/10.22244/rheedea.2020.30.03.01.

KUMAR-RAO, Arati. 2021. “No Honey, No Hives, but Solitary Bees Have Important Lives.” *Mongabay Series: Almost Famous Species*. ↗ https://india.mongabay.com/2021/03/no-honey-no-hives-but-solitary-bees-have-important-lives/. Accessed on June 27, 2024.

L

LATOUR, Bruno. 1993. *We Have Never Been Modern*. Translated by Catherine Porter. Harvard University Press.

LUBELLI, Barbara, Jeroen MOERMAN, Rita ESPOSITO, and Koen MULDER. 2021. “Influence of Brick and Mortar Properties on Bioreceptivity of Masonry: Results from Experimental Research.” *Construction and Building Materials* 266 (Part A): 121036. ↗ https://doi.org/10.1016/j.conbuildmat.2020.121036.

LUDWIG, Ferdinand, Wilfrid MIDDLETON, Friederike GALLENMÜLLER, Patrick ROGERS, and Thomas SPECK. 2019. “Living Bridges Using Aerial Roots of *Ficus elastica*: An Interdisciplinary Perspective.” *Scientific Reports* 9: 12226. ↗ https://doi.org/10.1038/s41598-019-48652-w.

M

MARDER, Michael. 2012. “Plant Intentionality and the Phenomenological Framework of Plant Intelligence.” *Plant Signalling and Behavior* 7 (11): 1365–72. ↗ https://www.ncbi.nlm.nih.gov/pmc/articles/PMC3548850/.

MARIANI, Manuela, and Patrick BARRON, eds. 2014. *Terrain Vague: Interstices at the Edge of the Pale*. Routledge.

MATHEW, Melvin. 2022. “A Hotel for Bees.” *Bangalore Mirror*, May 5. ↗ https://bangaloremirror.indiatimes.com/bangalore/others/a-hotel-for-bees/articleshow/91324593.cms. Accessed on April 17, 2024.

MATHUR, Anuradha, and Dilip DA CUNHA. 2001. *Mississippi Floods: Designing a Shifting Landscape*. Yale University Press.

MATHUR, Anuradha, and Dilip DA CUNHA. 2006. *Deccan Traverses: The Making of Bangalore’s Terrain*. Rupa and Company.

MATHUR, Anuradha, and Dilip DA CUNHA. 2009. *Soak: Mumbai in an Estuary*. Rupa and Company.

MATTHEWS, J. C., P. NAVASUMRIT, M. D. WRIGHT, et al. 2022. “Aerosol Mass and Size-Resolved Metal Content in Urban Bangkok, Thailand.” *Environmental Science and Pollution Research* 29: 79025–40. ↗ https://doi.org/10.1007/s11356-022-20806-w.

MATURANA, Humberto R., and Francisco J. VARELA. 1972. *Autopoiesis and Cognition: The Realization of the Living*. Boston Studies in the Philosophy and History of Science, 1st ed. Reidel.

McHARG, Ian Lennox. 1969. *Design with Nature*. Doubleday.

MERLEAU-PONTY, Maurice. 2002 (1958). *Phenomenology of Perception*. Translated by Kegan Paul. Routledge.

MIDDLETON, Wilfrid, Amin HABIBI, Sanjeev SHANKAR, and Ferdinand LUDWIG. 2020. “Characterizing Regenerative Aspects of Living Root Bridges.” *Sustainability* 12 (8): 3267. ↗ https://doi.org/10.3390/su12083267.

MINKJAN, Mark. 2016. “Spaces of Otherness: Ruins through a Feminist Lens.” *Failed Architecture*. ↗ https://failedarchitecture.com/spaces-of-otherness-ruins-through-a-feminist-lens/.

MITHAL Sonal, and Arul PAUL. 2024. *A Queer Reading of Nawabi Architecture and the Colonial Archive: Lucknow Queerscapes*. Routledge.

MITHAL, Sonal. 2019. Studio “Terrain-Vague Bricolage: Herbarium in an Abandoned Quarry at Champaner.” CEPT University.

MITHAL, Sonal. 2021. Studio “Ecotone: The Sentient Ruin—Ecological Recovery at an Abandoned Quarry at Champaner.” CEPT University.

MITHAL, Sonal. 2023. Studio “Staging Ecologies: Politics of Gender and Memory in Recovery of Qaiserbagh, Lucknow.” CEPT University.

MITHAL, Sonal. 2021. “Melding Matter: Feminist Ecologies for Architectural Thinking.” In *Gender and Academic Leadership in Architecture in India Symposium Proceedings*, edited by Kush Patel and Soumini Raja. Avni Institute of Design.

MITHAL, Sonal, and Seema KHANWALKAR. 2018. “Discovering the Abandoned and the Living: A Material Semiotic Reading of Heritage Textile Mills in Ahmedabad.” In *Cross-Inter-Multi-Trans: Proceedings of the 13th World Congress of the International Association for Semiotic Studies*, edited by Dario Martinelli. IASS Publications and International Semiotics Institute.

MYERS, Natasha. 2015. *Rendering Life Molecular: Models, Modelers, and Excitable Matter*. Duke University Press.

O

OOMMEN, Ansel. 2017. “Baubotanik: The Botanically Inspired Design System that Creates Living Buildings.” *ArchDaily*, September 14. ↗ https://www.archdaily.com/775884/baubotanik-the-botanically-inspired-design-system-that-creates-living-buildings.

OTERO-PAILOS, Jorge. 2009. *The Ethics of Dust*. Verlag der Buchhandlung Walther König.

OTERO-PAILOS, Jorge. 2010. “Ritual Cleaning.” *Perspecta* 43: 131–38. ↗ https://www.jstor.org/stable/41680278.

OWEN, Ceridwen. 2008. “Architecture between the Culture-Nature Dualism: A Case Study of Geoffrey Bawa’s Kandalama Hotel.” *Archnet: International Journal of Architectural Research* 2 (1): 40–56.

P

PATEL, Rameshkumar Jayantibhai. 2004. *Reuse of Old Mill Compounds in Eastern Part of Ahmedabad: A Land Use Modelling Approach*. Unpublished master’s thesis. Faculty of Urban Planning, CEPT University. ↗ http://hdl.handle.net/20.500.12725/14193.

PERINI, Katia, Maria CANEPA, Shany BARATH, Michael HENSEL, Anne MIMET, Surayyn Uthaya SELVAN, Enrica ROCCOTIELLO, Tina SELAMI, Defne Hensel SUNGUROGLU, Jakub TYC, Verena VOGLER, Wolfgang WEISSER, and Francesca MOSCA. 2021. “A Multi-species Design Approach to Building Envelope Design for Regenerative Urban Ecosystems." In *Responsive Cities: Design with Nature Symposium Proceedings*, edited by Areti Markoupoulou. Institut d'Arquitectura Avançada de Catalunya.

PLUMWOOD, Val. 1993. *Feminism and the Mastery of Nature*. Routledge.

PUIG DE LA BELLACASA, Maria. 2017. *Matters of Care: Speculative Ethics in More than Human Worlds*. University of Minnesota Press.

R

ROSENZWEIG, Michael L. 2003. *Win-Win Ecology: How the Earth's Species Can Survive in the Midst of Human Enterprise*. Oxford University Press.

S

SALAM, Aamirah, and Arpan DASGUPTA. 2021. "Tales of Traditions, Aspects of Adaptations and Stories of Sustenance of the Largest River Island of the World." *Elementary Education Online* 20 (1): 2084–99.

SCHEERBART, Paul. 2001. *The Gray Cloth: Paul Scheerbart's Novel on Glass Architecture*. MIT Press.

SELVAN, Surayyn Uthaya, Soultana Tanya SAROGLOU, Francesca MOSCA, Jakub TYC, Jens JOSCHINSKI, Mariasole CALBI, Verena VOGLER, Wolfgang WEISSER, Jacob Yasha GROBMAN, and Shany BARATH. 2023. "Multi-species Building Envelopes: Developing a Multi-criteria Design Decision-making Methodology for Cohabitation." *HUMAN-CENTRIC: Proceedings of the 28th CAADRIA Conference*, edited by Immanuel Koh, Dagmar Reinhardt, Mohammed Makki, and Mona Khakhar. ↗ https://doi.org/10.52842/conf.caadria.2023.2.643.

SEMKE, Rebecca. 2011. "Semnopithecus entellus" (Online), Animal Diversity Web. Accessed September 28, 2024 at ↗ https://animaldiversity.org/accounts/Semnopithecus_entellus/

SENTHIL, Aswin. 2021. "To Bee." CEPT University.

SERRES, Michel. 2011. *Malfeasance: Appropriation through Pollution?* Translated by Anne-Marie Feenberg-Dibon. Stanford University Press.

SHAH, Amrita. 2011. "Ethnography of an Indian City: Ahmedabad." In *The New Blackwell Companion to the City*, edited by Gary Bridge and Sophie Watson. Blackwell.

SHARMA, Pratibha, and Manpreet BINNER. 2020. "The Decline of Population of House Sparrow in India." *International Journal of Agricultural Science* 5.

SHERWILL, Walter Stanhope. 1851. *The Indian Opium, Its Mode of Preparation for the Chinese Market*. James Madden.

SOLÀ-MORALES RUBIÓ, Ignasi de. 1995. "Terrain Vague." In *Anyplace*, edited by Cynthia Davidson. MIT Press.

SOPER, Kate. 1995. *What Is Nature? Culture, Politics and the Non-human*. Blackwell.

SOUZA, Eduardo. 2022. "Giving Nature a Home in Cities: Bricks for Bees' Nests." *ArchDaily*, February 15. ↗ https://www.archdaily.com/976821/giving-nature-a-home-in-cities-bricks-for-bees-nests. Accessed June 27, 2024.

SPODEK, Howard. 1965. "The "Manchesterisation" of Ahmedabad." *The Economic Weekly*, March 13: 483–90.

STOLER, Ann Laura. 2008. "Imperial Debris: Reflections on Ruins and Ruination." *Cultural Anthropology* 23 (2): 191–219. ↗ https://www.jstor.org/stable/20484502.

T

TALENTO, Katia, Miguel AMADO, and José Carlos KULLBERG. 2020. "Quarries: From Abandoned to Renewed Places." *Land* 9 (5): 136. ↗ https://doi.org/10.3390/land9050136.

TSING, Anna Lowenhaupt. 2015. *The Mushroom at the End of the World: On the Possibility of Life in Capitalist Ruins*. Princeton University Press.

TSING, Anna Lowenhaupt, Heather SWANSON, Elaine GAN, and Nils BUBANDT, eds. 2017. *Arts of Living on a Dying Planet*. University of Minnesota Press.

U

UNESCO, Permanent Delegation of India. 2022. *Jingkieng Jri: Living Root Bridge Cultural Landscapes.* UNESCO. ↗ https://whc.unesco.org/en/tentativelists/6606/. Accessed on May 13, 2023.

UN DESA (United Nations Department of Economic and Social Affairs). 2018. "68% of the World Population Projected to Live in Urban Areas by 2050, Says UN." *UN DESA News*. Accessed on July 4, 2023. ↗ https://www.un.org/development/desa/en/news/population/2018-revision-of-world-urbanization-prospects.html.

USBR (US Department of the Interior Bureau of Reclamation). 2001. *Engineering Geology Field Manual*. Volume 2.

V

VAN DOOREN, Thom, and Deborah Bird ROSE. 2016. "Lively Ethnography." *Environmental Humanities* 8(1): 77–94. ↗ https://doi.org/10.1215/22011919-3527731.

VAN DOOREN, Thom, Eben KIRKSEY, and Ursula MÜNSTER. 2016. "Multispecies Studies: Cultivating Arts of Attentiveness." *Environmental Humanities* 8 (1): 1–23. ↗ https://doi.org/10.1215/22011919-3527695.

VARUGHESE, Jobin. 2011. *Birds in the City: Summer Observation, Number 6*. Landscape Environment Advancement Foundation.

VIGANO, Paola. 2016. *Territories of Urbanism: The Project as Knowledge Producer*. EPFL Press.

W

WRIGHT, Kate. 2014. "Becoming-With." *Environmental Humanities* 5(1): 277–81. ↗ https://doi.org/10.1215/22011919-3615514.

WRIGHT, Louise. 2021. "baracco+wright: garden house westernport." *afasiaarchzine*. ↗ https://afasiaarchzine.com/2021/04/baraccowright-garden-house-westernport/ Accessed on August 19, 2023.

Y

YULE, Henry. 1844. "Notes on the Kasia Hills, and People." *Journal of the Asiatic Society of Bengal* 13 (153): 612–31.

Z

ZUMTHOR, Peter. 2006. *Atmospheres*. Birkhäuser.

Image Credits

0	Fig 0.1	Illustration from Valih Musavi's Kabutarnama, 1788. British Library. I.O. ISLAMIC 4811.
	Fig 0.2	Opaque watercolor on paper, unknown artist, c. 1760s. Victoria and Albert Museum Collection. IS.97-1952.
	Fig 0.3	Pastel drawing, John A. Stuart, 2001.
	Fig 0.4	Digital collage, Céline Baumann, 2019.
	Fig 0.5a	Drawing, Jaikishore A., "Staging Ecologies" studio, 2023.
	Fig 0.5 b	Drawing, Jaikishore A., "Staging Ecologies" studio, 2023.
	Fig 0.6	Photograph, Akshar Gajjar, 2018.
1	Fig 1.1	Photograph, Sonal Mithal, 2023.
	Fig 1.2	Lithograph, Walter Sherwill, c. 1850. Wellcome Collection. 25043i.
	Fig 1.3	Digital collage, Roshita Sudhir, "Ecotone" studio, 2021.
	Fig 1.4	Digital collage, Lisa Therese, "Terrain-vague Bricolage" studio, 2019.
	Fig 1.5	Digital collage, Riddhi Verma, "Terrain-vague Bricolage" studio, 2019.
	Fig 1.6	Oil on canvas, Thomas Daniell, 1820. Yale Center for British Art. B1981.25.207.
	Fig 1.7	Drawing, Shivani Mehta, "Staging Ecologies" studio, 2023.
2	Fig 2.1	Photograph, "Terrain-vague Bricolage" studio, 2018.
	Fig 2.2	Photograph, Jorge Láscar, 2011.
	Fig 2.3	Photograph, Mikael Häggström, 2019.
	Fig 2.4	Satellite image, Google Earth, 2024.
	Fig 2.5	Photograph, Adarsh Patel, 2021.
	Fig 2.6	Photograph, Akshar Gajjar, 2024.
3	Fig 3.1–3.5	Drawing, Akshar Gajjar, 2021.
	Fig 3.6–3.7	Photograph, "Terrain-vague Bricolage" studio, 2018.
	Fig 3.8–3.9	Drawing, Lukas Ryffel, "Terrain-vague Bricolage" studio, 2018.
	Fig 3.10	Matrix, Lukas Ryffel, "Terrain-vague Bricolage" studio, 2018.
	Fig 3.11	Illustration, Simon Wurgler, "Terrain-vague Bricolage" studio, 2018.
	Fig 3.12–3.13	Illustration, Aswin Senthil and Karthik Nakkana, "Ecotone" studio, 2021.
	Fig 3.14	Photograph, "Terrain-vague Bricolage" studio, 2019.
	Fig 3.15	Illustration, Aswin Senthil and Karthik Nakkana, "Ecotone" studio, 2021.
	Fig 3.16	Photograph, "Terrain-vague Bricolage" studio, 2019.
	Fig 3.17	Photograph, "Terrain-vague Bricolage" studio, 2019.
	Fig 3.18	Drawing, Subham Pani and Aastha Wadhwa, "Ecotone" studio, 2021.
	Fig 3.19–3.22	Photograph, "Terrain-vague Bricolage" studio, 2019.
	Fig 3.23–3.29	Drawing, Harshil Amin, Nehal Jain, and Roshita Sudhir, "Ecotone" studio, 2021.

4

Fig 4.1	Photograph, Harikrishnan S., 2014.
Fig 4.2	Photograph, Joyce Hwang, 2015.
Fig 4.3	Photograph, Noshe, 2019.
Fig 4.4	Drawing, Jaikishore A., "Staging Ecologies" studio, 2023.
	inset Drawing, Jaikishore A., "Staging Ecologies" studio, 2023.
Fig 4.5	Drawing, Jaikishore A., "Staging Ecologies" studio, 2023.
Fig 4.6	Photograph, Rory Gardiner, 2013.
Fig 4.7	Photograph, Rory Gardiner, 2013.
Fig 4.8	Drawing, Eva Sussane Oberndorfer, "Terrain-vague Bricolage" studio, 2019.
Fig 4.9	Three-dimensional view, R&Sie(n), 2002.
Fig 4.10	Drawing, Aswin Senthil, "Ecotone" studio, 2021.
Fig 4.11	Drawing, Lukas Ryffel, "Terrain-vague Bricolage" studio, 2018.
Fig 4.12	Drawing, Lukas Ryffel, "Terrain-vague Bricolage" studio, 2018.
Fig 4.13	Drawing, Lukas Ryffel, "Terrain-vague Bricolage" studio, 2018.
Fig 4.14	Sketch, Casagrande Laboratory, 2003.
Fig 4.15	Photograph, Casagrande Laboratory, 2003.
Fig 4.16	Drawing, Aastha Wadhwa, "Ecotone" studio, 2021.
Fig 4.17	Drawing, Nehal Jain, "Ecotone" studio, 2021.
Fig 4.18	Drawing, Nehal Jain, "Ecotone" studio, 2021.

Acknowledgments

Living Together is a proposition to imagine architectures of living, caring, and growing together, and has been possible only through collective insights and the unwavering support of many.

This book has been generously supported by Professor Dr. Sarah Nichols, Director of Lab THEMA at the Swiss Federal Institute of Technology (EPFL), Lausanne. We are immensely grateful to Shailesh Patel, Nita Patel, Shiv Patel, and Michael Fingleton for their support. We would like to express our sincere appreciation to Professor Dr. Hélène Frichot for her deeply insightful foreword, in which she generously shares personal and scholarly reflections, adding depth and perspective to our book. We also acknowledge our respective universities, CEPT University and EPFL, for providing us with institutional support to write this book. We thank Dr. Karin Reisinger and Virginia Mannering for peer reviewing our manuscript and for their invaluable feedback. We extend our heartfelt gratitude to the architects, designers, and academicians who permitted us to publish images of their projects—Joyce Hwang, Tanja Lincke, Mauro Baracco and Louise Wright, François Roche, Stephanie Lavaux, Jean Navarro, Pascal Bertholio (R&Sie(n)), and Marco Casagrande—and to John Stuart for sharing images of his drawing. We thank Sian Phillips, Bridgeman Images, and Jack Glover Gunn, Victoria and Albert Images, for assisting with image publishing rights. We thank all students and teaching associates who were part of the studios at CEPT University that are featured in this book and whose participation in the studios has been foundational to this work: Gazal Nanwani (Teaching Associate), Jaikishore A. Shivani Mehta (Spring 2023); Ashwatha Chandran (Teaching Associate), Aastha Wadhwa, Amar Agarwal, Arun Cherian, Aswin Senthil, Harshil Amin, Karthik Nakkana, Kave Shinthu Prabakherran, Nehal Jain, Nitin Kademani, Roshita Sudhir, and Subham Pani (Spring 2021); Naomy Parikh (Teaching Associate), Riddhi Varma, and Lisa Therese (Monsoon 2019); Kruti Shah (Teaching Associate), Aradhana K. Adnan Makda, Chirag Meghani, Eva Susanne Oberndorfer, Khushboo Makwana, Niharika Jadav, Noam Keidar, Prutha Barot, and Sudarshana (Spring 2019); Aashini Sheth, Aastha Maheshwari, Dhruv Patel, Itziar Luzuriaga, Krupa Patel, Lukas Ryffel, Milan Desai, Pedro Gomez, Setu Sherawala, and Simon Wurgler (Spring 2018).

We thank Baharak Tajbakhsh, our Editor at Birkhäuser, for meticulously coordinating the publication process and patiently responding to our queries. Special thanks to Nils Havelka for his meticulous feedback and constructive input, which significantly helped the book. We thank Birkhäuser for giving our book a home.

This book is evidence of the support our family and friends gave us during our writing journey. Sumesh Modi and Sanskriti have been the endurance we constantly needed. Shailesh Gajjar, Shital Gajjar, and Sakshar have provided unceasing faith and support since the inception of the project.

Imprint

Copy editing	Max Bach
	On behalf of the publisher
Acquisitions Editor	Baharak Tajbakhsh
Production Editor	Amelie Solbrig
Layout, cover design and typesetting	arc ↗ www.arc-gestaltung.de
Paper	Kamiko Fly Suna, 100 g/m²
Image Editing	prints professional, Berlin
Printing	Beltz Grafische Betriebe
	Published with the support of the Swiss National Science Foundation (SNSF). This publication has been peer reviewed according to SNSF standards.
Library of Congress Control Number	2025935655
Bibliographic information	published by the German National Library The German National Library lists this publication in the Deutsche Nationalbibliografie; detailed bibliographic data are available on the Internet at ↗ http://dnb.dnb.de.
creative commons	This work is licensed under the Creative Commons Attribution-NonCommercial-NoDerivatives 4.0 International License. For details go to ↗ http://creativecommons.org/licenses/by-nc-nd/4.0/.
ISBN	978-3-0356-2815-9
e-ISBN (PDF)	978-3-0356-2825-8 Open Access
DOI	↗ https://doi.org/10.1515/9783035628258
©	2025 Sonal Mithal, Akshar Gajjar
Published by	Birkhäuser Verlag GmbH, Basel Im Westfeld 8, 4055 Basel, Switzerland Part of Walter de Gruyter GmbH, Berlin/Boston
	The book is published open access at ↗ www.degruyter.com.
	www.birkhauser.com
	Questions about General Product Safety Regulation productsafety@degruyterbrill.com
	9 8 7 6 5 4 3 2 1

FSC www.fsc.org MIX Papier | Fördert gute Waldnutzung FSC® C089473